About the Author

Rosemary Hollis has worked in academia and the 'think tank' community in London and in Washington D.C. She was Director of the Olive Tree Scholarship Programme for Palestinians and Israelis (2008-16) and Professor of Middle East Policy Studies (2012-18) at City, University of London. Before that, Rosemary was Director of Research (2005-08) and Head of the Middle East Programme (1995-2005) at Chatham House (the Royal Institute of International Affairs) in London. From 1990-95 she was Head of the Middle East Programme at RUSI (the Royal United Services Institute for Defence Studies). She gained her PhD in Political Science from George Washington University in Washington, DC, where she also taught for several years in the 1980s. She has an MA in War Studies (1975) and BA in History (1974) from King's College, University of London. She has published extensively on issues to do with the international politics of the Middle East and conflicts in the region.

BY THE SAME AUTHOR

Britain and the Middle East in the 9/11 Era

Israel and the Palestinians: Israeli Policy Options, with Mark A. Heller.

Jordanian-Palestinian Relations: Where To? with Mustafa Hamarneh and Khalil Shikaki.

Israel on the Brink of Decision: Division, Unity and Crosscurrents in the Israeli Body Politic.

Journal articles and chapters in edited volumes, including:

'**Europe in the Middle East**', in Louise Fawcett, ed., *The International Relations of the Middle East* (Oxford: OUP, 5 editions).

'**Palestine and the Palestinians in British Political Elite Discourse: From "The Palestine Problem" to "The Two-State Solution,"**' *International Relations*. Vol. 30(1).

A comprehensive list of Dr Hollis's publications can be found at **www.rosemaryhollis.co.uk**

SURVIVING THE STORY

The Narrative Trap In Israel and Palestine

ROSEMARY HOLLIS

Red Hawk Books
London and Swansea

Red Hawk Books is an imprint of Red Hawk Media Ltd
whose addresses can be found at
www.redhawkmedia.co.uk

First published by Red Hawk Books in 2019
A CIP record for this book is available from the British Library
978-1-9160843-1-5
Cover design and layout by Adam Evans
Original photography by Yoav Galai

For my father

Contents

If I was us, I wouldn't start from here

In 2018, to mark the 20th anniversary of the signing of Northern Ireland's Good Friday peace Agreement, I was asked to write a poem for a public space. This poem was commissioned for The Poetry Jukebox, a beautiful blue periscope of a thing which rises from the ground outside the Crescent Arts Centre in Belfast, and affords all kinds of perspectives. When I settled to writing the piece I found that I was actually sitting down with two conflicts in mind: the 'Troubles', of course – that most recent episode of violence and unrest in my native Northern Ireland which has occupied so much of my lifetime and, to some extent, defined it; and the Middle East conflict, as I have been brought into contact with it through my years working on the Olive Tree programme. And while obviously there are particular references to Northern Ireland in the poem, the truth is that throughout the writing process – from the title, through the core theme to the end thought – I was holding both conflicts in mind, and trying to speak to them both. Here then, as my contribution to Rosemary's book, is *If I Was Us, I Wouldn't Start From Here*. I dedicate it here to her; to all the colleagues – from City University, from Northern Ireland and elsewhere – I worked with on the Olive Tree programme over many years. And, above all, I dedicate it here to the students, from whose courage and openness and stories I learned so much.

Damian Gorman

If I was us, I wouldn't start from here

Especially in a broken home like ours,
Where broken floors and windows feed the cold,
Each generation has a sacred task:
To tell a better story than it was told.

For we are reared by stories in such places,
Clawing through the bitter draughts of these
For something we can truly get a hold of
That seems to help us off our shattered knees.

The kind of myth my generation supped
Was, 'We have better heroes than they've got.
For ours are much more decent – to a fault.
And, if we've a rotten apple, they've the Rot.'

Our steps now are, at best, precise and formal
Like dressage horses going nowhere well.
Our peace a thing we part-baked in the 90s
And left to prove, and got used to the smell.

Yet even in this half-peace we are living
Where death is only half-dead, I am sure
That we could learn to change our tunes completely,
But if I was us I wouldn't start from here.

If I was us I wouldn't start from here
For Here's a swamp we've stood in for too long.
We haven't kept our heads above the water,
And haven't seen a thing where we have gone

And we should fly now – frightened for our children -
Kick off the bottom; rush towards the air;
And break the water into different daylight
And gasp; and say what we can see from there.

For especially in a broken home like ours,
Where broken floors and windows feed the cold,
Each generation has a sacred task:
To tell a better story than it was told

A story made, as honey is in bees,
From things that we have found outside ourselves.

Damian Gorman

Introduction

This book explores the role played by group or national narratives in the intensification of conflict. It also relates how one specific instance of cross-conflict dialogue helped to reveal the enduring strength and emotional appeal of such narratives in conflicts about identity. Group narratives reinforce differences between warring parties and work against notions of equality with one another. As such, they also militate against pragmatism and compromise.

In what follows, several commonly held assumptions about conflicts in general and the usefulness of dialogue are examined and several of them debunked. Alternative insights and ways of understanding are proposed. The work draws on my own observations and practical experience working with people in conflict, and in particular it recounts lessons that I learned from working with Palestinian and Israeli students who participated in an intensive cross-conflict dialogue exercise undertaken at City, University of London between 2004 and 2016 (the Olive Tree Programme).

With respect to this programme, I must clarify that I did not initiate it. Instead I took it over in 2008, by which point it was in a state of near collapse, largely because its original goals had proved unrealistic. Well-meaning attempts to persuade ordinary people, from opposite sides of a conflict, to reconcile their differences – in the absence of a commitment by their respective political leaders to do so – are bound to meet with disappointment. In fact, such attempts can actually increase animosity.

Being aware of this, when I took over the Olive Tree I completely reconfigured it, changing it from a would-be 'peace programme' into a purely educational exercise in which the students could learn more about the forces at work in their situation 'back home.' As a result, the students and I were able to discover how their respective national narratives act as drivers toward ever deeper conflict. The findings of our endeavours are the subject of this book and, as will become clear, they have general applicability and can be instructive in other contexts.

All conflicts, I contend, should not be understood as aberrations or departures from a peaceful 'norm' that otherwise prevails, even though it may be tempting to do so. Those of us who have enjoyed decades of peaceful coexistence with our neighbours in Western Europe since the end of the Second World War cannot assume that peace is the norm when we are not directly embroiled in war. Instead, tensions and conflicts, be they between individuals, groups, or minorities and majorities, are ever present, even though these may not turn to violence across whole societies. The norm is the coexistence of relative harmony *and* disharmony at the societal level, war *and* peace at the regional and global level, all the time.

Competing national and sectarian narratives embody within them group identities and all of us grow up with one or another such narrative. Our power to opt out or choose an alternative story or identity is limited. Thus, examination of such narratives holds the key to better understanding the dynamic at work. In making this contention I depart from and challenge the dominant thinking and theories about international and civil conflicts that 'problematize' or isolate the conflict as the object of study.

In the case of international conflicts, such approaches typically focus on the material issues in dispute and look for compromise between protagonists on those issues as the key to conflict resolution. Thus, the approach most commonly proposed by third parties for resolving the Israeli-Palestinian conflict, has been to call on the protagonists to 'make the painful territorial compromises required' to settle the dispute. Yet this is to assume that the warring parties can step outside the stories that define them.

In the case of civil conflicts, authority figures will frequently propose the integration of minorities through their assimilation into a presumed mainstream. Thus the line adopted by the British government toward migrant integration has been to enjoin acceptance of so-called 'British values'. Before the 'Brexit' phenomenon created new divisions, these values were defined as 'mutual respect and tolerance', 'democracy', 'individual liberty' and 'the rule of law'.[1] Yet, how a person understands those values will depend on what story of the British Isles a person has been brought up with and their experience of 'Britishness' (as opposed to 'Frenchness' or 'Iraqiness' for example).

The claim here is that a separation cannot be made between the protagonists in a conflict – and how they understand themselves in relation to 'the other' – and the pursuit or presence of conflict. Conflict is present, even when not manifest at a level of violence commonly designated as 'war', within the

---

[1] www.gov.uk/government/news/guidance-on-promoting-british-values-in-schools-published

narratives that define groups and difference. What is at stake in a conflict is the self-understanding or self-identification of the protagonists *and* their power relations. Assertion of power or dominance cannot remove differences, only exacerbate them.

Group 'narratives' are defined here as stories or explications that draw on collective memories, historical experiences, seminal texts and myths from which may be derived meanings and values, that define the group – who they are and who they are not. The construction, development and espousal of the narratives juxtapose self and other, in-group and out-group, affirmation and approbation, vindication and blame.

Competing or divergent narratives also enshrine power relations between groups. This observation is well explored in the literature on the discourses of imperialism, where narratives serve the coloniser to justify dominance.[2] In the post-colonial context, however, discussions about national narratives tend to depict these as mirror images of aggression and victimhood rooted in the past, but not valid in the present. This has been the case in analyses of the dynamics of the Arab-Israeli conflict writ large, wherein Israeli claims of victimhood are discounted as a hangover from the era of Nazism in Europe and pogroms in Russia, and Arab claims of oppression are dismissed as harking back to the imperial past. Yet both sets of claims live on and acquire new permutations in the present. They also undermine the myth that prevails among Europeans today that they are mere bystanders to developments in the Middle East.

It was the Europeans who remade the Middle East and North Africa on the basis of their notions of nationalism and the 'nation-state'. Following the collapse of the Ottoman Empire at the end of the First World War, it was the British and French who divided up the Arab World into separate states and dependencies. The French presided over the separation of Lebanon from Syria. The British presided over the foundation of a Jewish 'national home' in Palestine, invented Iraq and founded the Hashemite Kingdom of Jordan. The lines they drew on the map cut across pre-existing social, tribal, ethnic and sectarian identities and commercial connections. The rulers of the newly created Arab states used a combination of nationalism, sectarianism, anti-imperialism, an-

---

[2] See for example Doty, R. L. (1996) *Imperial Encounters* Minneapolis & London: University of Minnesota Press; and Ghandour, Z. (2010) *A Discourse on Domination in Mandate Palestine: Imperialism, Property and Insurgency* Oxford: Routledge.

ti-Zionism, socialism or monarchy, and competition with one another to claim legitimacy. Meanwhile, the founders of Israel embraced Jewish national identity as the basis of self-determination and their answer to centuries of discrimination faced by Jews in Europe.

For the duration of the Cold War the United States and the Soviet Union forged clientelist relationships with regional governments, cemented with arms sales and military training. Following the end of the Cold War, with Russian acquiescence, the US, aided by the forces of several European and Arab states, reversed the Iraqi invasion of Kuwait in 1991. Thereafter, the US adopted an approach it called 'dual containment' of both Iraq and Iran that endured until the attacks of 9/11 prompted US President George W. Bush to declare a 'war on terror'. Both these conceptualisations ('dual containment' and 'the war on terror') exemplify conflict narratives that distinguish between 'us' and 'them', with dynamics of their own. Several Arab governments and Israel embraced these meta narratives and combined them with their own 'home-grown' versions.

There followed the invasion of Iraq, which reinvented and exacerbated sectarian animosities in that country and beyond. Meanwhile, the European Union pursued a 'Neighbourhood Policy' that enshrined the promotion of 'European values' of liberal market capitalism and human rights in Arab states around the Mediterranean. The mismatch between the reforms the Europeans thought they were enabling and the persistence of dictatorial rule on the receiving end was made manifest in the Arab uprisings of 2011.[3] European and US efforts to frame their subsequent military intervention in Libya invoked the UN Convention on 'the Responsibility to Protect,' but delivered the fall of Qadhafi and thereafter civil war. Absent consensus in the UN Security Council on whether and how to intervene in Syria, that country descended into a war of near total destruction, with both regional and international powers backing different factions, and all of them claiming the moral high ground.

Lastly, the emergence of the so-called Islamic State (IS) in Syria and Iraq attracted hundreds of volunteers from across the region and Europe, obliging European governments to rethink their policies on migrant integration at home, while deploying their airpower to defeat the advance of IS in the region.

---

[3] See Hollis, R. (2012) 'No friend of democratisation: Europe's role in the genesis of the "Arab Spring"' *International Affairs* 88(1); and Hollis, R. (2016) 'The Role of the European Union' in Sverre Lodgaard, ed. *External Powers and the Arab Spring* Oslo: Scandinavian Academic Press.

When the arrival in Europe of ever more refugees, from North Africa, Syria and beyond, presented the EU with an unprecedented challenge to accommodate these desperate people, the political fortunes of European nationalist or 'nativist' movements were boosted.

My point here is that Europeans cannot claim that events in the Middle East are not their business or that the forces at work there, including competing nationalist and sectarian movements, are alien to the European experience. Part of the problem, in fact, is that European identity is rooted in an understanding of the past which juxtaposes a European or 'Western' self and the Oriental 'other'. The 'nativist' voices in Europe claim a racial (white verses brown) and religious (Christian versus Muslim) divide is threatening social harmony and the relative prosperity of Europe, to which the response must be a hardening of borders and suppression of diversity within.

Intriguingly, across the political spectrum in Europe, the Israeli-Palestinian conflict is treated as a kind of surrogate battleground for working out their respective theories about the human condition. Advocates of one side or the other invest great passion and righteousness in defending the rights and needs of the party with whom they most identify. Debates about the conflict are more often heated and emotional than calm and reflective, no doubt in large part because the origins of the conflict are as rooted in European history as they are in that of the Middle East. And contemporary concepts of European identity which boast a particular religious heritage draw on Biblical stories and records of the Roman Empire, as well as later stories about the Crusades.

In making reference to past eras, my purpose is simply to remind that our national and group narratives do draw on the past, albeit selectively and with modern embellishments. And since that past encompasses all the shores of the Mediterranean, it makes no sense to set about trying to understand the present without an awareness of a *shared* past that has linked Europe and the Middle East for centuries. Further, conflicts and tensions as well as periods of harmony between different communities, encompassed by successive empires, have been the norm. And finally, that norm has persisted into the age of competing nationalisms and the drivers of conflict include competing group narratives that define 'us and them'.

It is against this background that I wish to explore further the role of group narratives in deepening conflicts. The Israeli-Palestinian conflict provides the context for this exploration. This is not because I have theories about how to resolve it, nor because I deem this conflict uniquely fascinating. It just happens that I had the opportunity to study this particular conflict most intensively and in the company of some of the protagonists. Also, I see it as a cautionary tale, with relevance elsewhere, about the consequences of overinvestment in exclusivist group identities and narratives. It illustrates how two groups or identities can become so trapped in their respective narratives, that they cannot define themselves except in distinction from the other. Before embarking, however, several points require some clarification.

First, the material discussed in this book derives from the Olive Tree Programme. The insights it generated were not foreseen, but came about as it were serendipitously. The Palestinian and Israeli students awarded scholarships under this programme generated the main findings during the course of their group interactions. It was not specifically planned that way, but, as psychologists and therapists who work with groups will attest, how learning and discovery takes place in a group is not the same as how an individual, with or without the guidance of a supervisor or facilitator, advances their understanding. In other words, the main planks in the arguments advanced in this book came out of group interactions between conflict protagonists. As such, these arguments have a potency that could not be replicated through any amount of individual study and research.

Second, given the findings of the group interactions, I identified some hypotheses about the narratives that I wanted to test further. This I did in the form of a survey or questionnaire to which not only students and alumni of the Olive Tree Programme responded, but also the members of two 'comparator' groups, one Israeli and the other Palestinian. These were made up of respondents of similar age and profile to the Olive Tree scholars, but who had not had group interactions or intensive dialogue with their respective enemies. The details of the survey are explained in Chapter 2 and the responses collected are quoted at length in Chapters 3 to 7, to illustrate the arguments made and underpin the conclusions reached.

As the survey responses demonstrated, cross-conflict dialogue, at the civil society or grassroots level, can change minds on some aspects of the conflict, but not to such a degree as to substantiate claims that dialogue is a reliable route to agreement or peace. Far more significant was the discovery that the competing Israeli and Palestinian narratives are so ingrained and firmly held as to defy major reconsideration through contact with the enemy. This book is not, therefore, an exposition on the value of dialogue, though, I contend, it was helpful to the participants in the Olive Tree in so far as it enabled them to review their personal options for how to proceed with their lives.

Chapter 1 is devoted to a review of the literature on dialogue exercises in general and in the Israeli-Palestinian context in particular. The inspiration for almost all such exercises has been 'the contact hypothesis' propounded by American social psychologist Gordon Allport in the 1950s. Here his theories are examined with the aid of a compelling critique of the methodology used by Allport and his disciples, published by H. D. Forbes, a professor of political science at the University of Toronto, in 1997. The discussion then moves to a review of several works recounting the experiences of facilitators and participants in dialogue exercises between Israelis and Palestinians, focusing on those undertaken at the grassroots or 'people-to-people' level. With some notable exceptions, most of these have met with disappointment, for reasons which are instructive in themselves.

Chapter 2 explains the terms on which the Olive Tree Programme was convened during my time as director, and what it did and did not accomplish for the participants. As explained there, this programme was exceptional in many respects, not least because it took place in London, over an extended period and within a university setting. It is unlikely to be replicated on a significant scale, if at all, and so the learnings it generated are especially worth recording for general reference. Chapter 2 also provides an explanation of the survey I designed, how it was conducted, the questions posed and to whom.

The subsequent chapters then deal thematically with the insights I gleaned from the Olive Tree experience on the drivers of conflict and the role of competing parallel national narratives in determining its trajectory. Chapter 3 discusses identity construction and the institutionalisation of hate and blame. Chapter 4 is devoted to an explication of the 'mainstream' national narratives of the parties to the conflict, as articulated by some of the protagonists. In this as other chapters, the perceptions and accounts of Olive Tree participants are compared and contrasted with those of the 'comparator' group Israelis and Palestinians – all of similar age and educational qualifications to the Olive Tree scholars, but who had not been exposed to 'the other' to the same extent.

In Chapter 5 the discussion turns to the role of 'facts on the ground' and 'the occupation' in framing perceptions of self and other. The asymmetry in power relations between the conflicting parties cannot be ignored or downplayed in any analysis of the conflict. That asymmetry features prominently in the narratives and identities of both sides. Chapter 6 examines what is cynically termed 'the peace business', looking specifically at perceptions of the 'Oslo Process'. This was understood in largely positive terms by Israeli respondents, but dismissed as a mechanism for perpetuating the occupation by most of the Palestinians. Chapter 7 examines the ways in which Palestinian and Israeli participants in this study perceive the future.

The Conclusions at the end of the book include a summary of all the findings and how they came about. The reader may wish to turn to the Conclusions even before reading the intervening chapters, to gain an overview and thence determine how much to delve into the details provided in those chapters.

Among the conclusions reached is that Israeli identity is equated with citizenship of their own state while Palestinian identity is equated with statelessness and dispossession. When asked what they want now, all the Palestinians surveyed said they want freedom and an end to occupation. They said they want 'the same as what the Israelis want for themselves'. Those Israelis who went through three years of dialogue with the Palestinians had grasped this very clearly.

However, not one of the other Israelis surveyed for this study had anything other than theories about what the Palestinians want now and none of them mentioned freedom or an end to occupation as a Palestinian aspiration. Instead they assumed the Palestinians were focused on what they would do, if they could, to Jewish Israelis. Meanwhile, asked what the Israelis want now, Israeli respondents said peace and quiet and international respect. By contrast, the Palestinians surveyed thought that the Israelis must want to continue the occupation otherwise they would have found a way to end it. They also assumed the Israelis want 'to keep it all' and for the Palestinians to give up resistance.

The asymmetry in Israeli-Palestinian relations – and the persistence of the occupation – is dealt with very differently in their respective narratives. The co-existence of their competing national narratives both drives and entrenches the conflict. They operate in parallel and only partially intersect. Each enshrines a positive depiction of 'self' that relies on a negative construction of 'the other' and they embody irreconcilable understandings of 'the facts'. The narratives are also dynamic and drive the protagonists to greater extremes of behaviour toward the other.

On a more general note, thanks to the intensive work undertaken by the Palestinians and Israelis involved in the Olive Tree Programme, together with the insights gleaned from the survey undertaken for this book, it has been possible to discover more about the role of group narratives in driving conflict, not only in that setting, but more widely. Hence, as will be seen, our national narratives can trap us into acting out imperatives embedded in those narratives in an unreflecting way. The main message here is therefore about discerning what I am calling 'the narrative trap' and thereby finding or retrieving a level of agency, rather than simply acting out 'The Story' we are told by the powers that be.

1

Cross-Conflict Dialogue – Theory and Practice

Dialogue between people or groups in conflict is not an automatic route to peace or agreement between them. On the contrary, the participants may use dialogue to pursue conflicting agendas. The starting point for understanding this is to accept that conflict is normal and ever present, to varying degrees, in relations between people and groups, as is also acceptance, agreement and harmony, to varying degrees. Consider, for example, relations between couples, siblings, parents and children. The norm in their relations will likely encompass a range of emotions and drivers, including tension, rivalry, competition, resentment, affection, dependence or co-dependence, respect and what is generally understood as love and quite possibly hate.

Thanks to the literary classics and of course much social science research, in particular psychology, it is possible to comprehend the coexistence of seemingly conflicting emotions in all of us and to understand relationships between people and groups as determined by complex mixtures of emotions on the part of all concerned. Learning to identify the emotional 'baggage' which we bring to our interactions with others, be they close family members, partners, friends, colleagues, strangers or those we experience or have learned to see as enemies, can be enabled by psychotherapy. Such learning can be attained through individual or one-on-one conversations with a therapist, or through group discussions facilitated by a third party. In the former case, the learning sought will occur at the individual level, putting the person concerned in touch with their own emotions and thence, ideally, enabling them to manage those emotions rather than acting on them without pausing for reflection. In facilitated group exercises, learning can occur at both the individual and group level, putting participants in touch with both their own emotions and their group identities. The goal is to enable all concerned to find a level of agency in the face of emotional drivers that otherwise determine their choices.

This, at least, is how I understand the potential value of facilitated cross-conflict dialogue between strangers and/or enemies. Such exercises afford the participants an opportunity to identify and reflect upon the emotions driving their individual and group actions and reactions. Crucially, though, simply putting together people from opposing sides in a simmering conflict or hot war, will not necessarily free up the participants from acting out their animosities and resentments within the exercise. The extent to which they will attain a deeper level of understanding of what is going on will depend on how the exercise is configured, how it is facilitated and what ground rules and goals are identified.

For a clear articulation of my meaning here, I refer the reader to the works of John Winslade and Gerald Monk, leading figures in 'the narrative therapy movement'.[1] The main focus of the work of Winslade and Monk has been on conflict resolution between divorcing couples and within organizations. However, the approach and tools they have developed have potential for adoption in the mediation of political, ethnic and sectarian conflicts. They emphasise the importance of the stories or narratives of conflict protagonists in shaping experiences, constructing relationships and influencing mind-sets. Taking issue with those professionals in the social sciences who see stories as unreliable fabrications or irrelevances, they see them as key to understanding conflict. To dismiss the stories is to miss 'the work done by stories to *construct* realities, not just to report them, apparently inaccurately' [their emphasis]:

> Rather than moving as quickly as one can away from stories and toward an emphasis on what is factual, objective, and patterned, we believe there is much to be gained by staying with the stories themselves, inquiring into the work that they do, and experimenting with how these stories might be reshaped in order to transform relationships.[2]

From these insights I do not deduce that reality is 'all in the mind', and that therefore, for example, the Israeli occupation of the West Bank is merely a perception of the Palestinians. Rather, I deduce that the Israelis are in occupation of Palestinian land because, in the popular narrative promoted by their

---

[1] See John Winslade and Gerald Monk (2008) *Practicing Narrative Mediation: Loosening the Grip of Conflict* San Fransisco: Josse-Bass, a Wiley imprint; and John Winslade and Gerald Monk (2000) *Narrative Mediation: A New Approach to Conflict Resolution* San Fransisco: Josse-Bass, a Wiley imprint.

[2] Winslade and Monk (2008) p.2.

government, that land belongs to them, not the Palestinians. Thus, the narrative is more than simply a claim or disputed perspective – it is also a driver of Israeli actions. Similarly, Palestinians understand themselves as the indigenous people of Palestine who have progressively lost their land to another people. The claims of the latter do not change their experience of what it means to be Palestinian.

In any case, I shall have much more to say about narratives as drivers of conflict in subsequent chapters. Here, the purpose of introducing the subject is to illuminate what can be achieved in cross-conflict dialogue if it is understood as a context within which the participants can be alerted to the role of narratives in enshrining both group identity and imperatives. A person who grows up in the context of one group cannot easily reappraise their identity or choose a different narrative.

Each narrative is internally coherent and logical. In order to realise its particularities requires experiencing dissonance between it and another narrative. As social anthropologist Edward Hall describes so eloquently,[3] for people in one culture to grasp how bound and conditioned by their culture they are, they have to experience culture clash. Without that, they will tend to assume that the world they live in is normal, rational and natural. By contrast, those who have lived outside the country or community they grew up in will likely have learned as much about themselves and their native community as about the new one in which they subsequently find themselves.

It is in accordance with this realisation that a case for cross-conflict dialogue as a learning exercise can be built. Such exercises afford the opportunity to learn about oneself and one's own group identity as much as it does to learn about the other. In the process a sense of the existence of two or more firmly held and formative narratives can emerge. That experience is likely to be very disorientating and frightening. It may lead to the realisation that no single narrative will prevail or eradicate the others, not by war or through a peace agreement. And opposing group narratives cannot be amalgamated into a single new one built from scratch. To think so would be to misunderstand what group narratives are all about.

With the foregoing discussion as background, what follows is a discussion and critique of a range of theories and assumptions commonly made about cross-conflict dialogue. Drawing on my own experience and that of others who

---

[3] Edward Hall (1977) *Beyond Culture* New York: Anchor Books.

have written about their discoveries, I shall also identify four key features of so-called 'people-to-people' (P2P) dialogue at the civil society level.[4] First, such grassroots dialogue should not be confused with formal negotiations. Second, P2P encounters may change the participants in the exercise, but cannot transform society. Third, to be meaningful, these endeavours require facing up to asymmetries in the power relations between the participants, rather than pretending all those involved enjoy equal status. And finally, therefore, such exercises mean recognising group identity as well as enabling individual agency and self-awareness.

People-to-People (P2P) Dialogue vs. Formal Negotiations

Dialogue is not the same as negotiation. The latter is a requirement for conflict resolution and dialogue may prepare the ground for negotiation. Yet it is a mistake to assume that the goal of any or all dialogue must be agreement or conflict resolution. To espouse such a goal may actually undermine the potential of dialogue to explore differences and gain an understanding of 'the other', because if participants think they have to use the conversation to advance their position, to make gains, they are less likely to be in listening mode.

The distinction between dialogue as a learning exercise, and negotiation as a means to reach agreement, becomes clear when we consider the difference between, on the one hand, formal meetings between top level officials or diplomats tasked with negotiating a deal with counterparts from another country or organisation, and, on the other hand, cross-conflict dialogue exercises at the grassroots level. In the latter case the participants are not in a position to negotiate or agree a deal, and even if they try to do so, any agreement reached would not be binding.

In the conduct of international relations, a distinction is made between three levels or types of interaction between conflict protagonists. Formal meetings between senior officials are designated as Track I diplomacy and that is the level at which formal agreements can be made. One level down from such top-level interactions, preparations may have been made through discussions

---

[4] The term 'people-to-people' derives from Annex VI of *Oslo II: The Interim Agreement on the West Bank and Gaza Strip* of 1995, which called for 'cooperation in enhancing the dialogue and relations between the two peoples through a people-to-people program'. The EU was to adopt the same term, 'People to People', for the first of its initiatives to promote civil society dialogue and cooperative projects between Israelis, Palestinians and Jordanians in 1998.

between individuals with *access* to official decision-makers, but with no remit to speak in their name, and this is known as Track II diplomacy.[5] At this level meetings are typically conducted in secret, away from public gaze and media attention, to explore the possibilities for conflict resolution at an unofficial level. The task of the participants at this level is to test out possibilities and then feed back to decision-makers the findings of their endeavours.

The Middle East Peace Process (MEPP) has involved multiple Track II exercises over the years, the most famous of which was the back-channel discussions instigated by the Norwegians which laid the ground for the Oslo Accords. In that instance, the participants had the ear and the trust of their respective political leaders, but no power to seal a formal agreement. Thus, when the parties to the secret Oslo meetings had mapped out the basis for a deal, responsibility for formalising the Declaration of Principles (the first Oslo Accord or Oslo I) passed to the official leaderships of the Palestine Liberation Organisation (PLO) and the Israeli Government. It was Yasser Arafat, Chairman of the PLO, and PLO official Ahmed Qurei who signed the first Oslo Accord on behalf of the Palestinians, together with Israeli Prime Minister Yitzhak Rabin and Foreign Minister Shimon Peres on behalf of the Israelis. They did so at a public ceremony presided over by the US President Bill Clinton on the White House lawn in September 1993. Of these five individuals, only Qurei had been present during the secret Oslo talks.

The Oslo dialogue was not the only Track II endeavour to have secretly explored the parameters for an Israeli-Palestinian agreement prior to September 1993. But Oslo was the one that the respective leaderships endorsed. There have been many more Track II exercises since 1993, bringing together Palestinian and Israeli interlocutors with varying degrees of access to their official leaders and influence within their respective communities, but none of them have resulted in official deals. Such deals that have been made since Oslo I, such as the Gaza-Jericho Agreement (1994), Oslo II (1995) and the Wye River Memorandum (1998), were negotiated between officials.

There are parallels here with the various Track II diplomatic efforts that preceded the conclusion of the Good Friday Agreement that marked a major turning point in the Northern Ireland peace process in 1998. There were sim-

---

[5] Kaye, D. D. (2007) *Talking to the Enemy: Track Two Diplomacy in the Middle East and South Asia.* Santa Monica, CA: RAND Corporation.

ilar efforts, over many years, which preceded the signing of a deal between the Colombian government and the Farc rebels in 2016, some directly involving officials. Yet the only deals that count are those formally and publicly signed and even then such deals may not last if not embraced by the people, the rank and file, on both sides. It is in this connection that P2P dialogue can make a difference to the sustainability of an official agreement, but P2P is not the same as either Track I or Track II Diplomacy. Some choose to call P2P dialogue Track III Diplomacy. Crucially though, by itself P2P cannot substitute for a lack of commitment to ending a conflict at the official Track I level and unless it were to take place on a massive scale, P2P cannot be used to mobilise a population and thereby exert pressure on leaders to change their preferences (as explicated in the next section of this chapter).

To summarise, what can be expected of cross-conflict dialogue at the grassroots level is context dependent. If a peace deal has been signed and the leaderships on both sides are committed to this, P2P can serve to build grassroots support for that deal. However, if the leaderships of one or both sides in a conflict are not invested in resolving the causes of conflict, then P2P cannot substitute for leadership engagement. Not only is P2P not a suitable arena for pursuing negotiations i.e. conflict resolution, but also P2P will simply become a setting for the pursuit of disagreement and conflict, rendering all participants frustrated and quite probably alienated.

Consequently, when there is no commitment to peace at the official leadership level, the potential utility of P2P is very different from when there is such commitment. Following Oslo I in 1993 it was plausible to represent P2P dialogue as a mechanism for building grassroots support for the deals made at the leadership level. However, when the peace process collapsed, people at the grassroots faced the choice of either going against their leaders or closing ranks with them in support of their national cause.

Jon Hanssen-Bauer, the man appointed by the Norwegian government to help design and direct an official P2P programme to bolster public support for the official Oslo process in the 1990s, makes it very clear that he blames developments in the formal peace process at the top political level for 'what went wrong' with grassroots dialogue. As he recounts:

The initiative came from the chief negotiators in the secret Oslo channel. They were concerned about how little Palestinians knew about Israelis and

CROSS-CONFLICT DIALOGUE – THEORY AND PRACTICE

vice versa. The Oslo agreement was the result of elite negotiations, and the negotiators wanted to bridge the gap between them and their publics. By embarking on the programme, the authorities wanted to provide legitimacy to those on both sides who wanted to meet and cooperate after the Parties had signed their mutual recognition.[6]

Design of the programme was carried out by a team comprising Norwegian representatives and two NGOs, one Palestinian and one Israeli. The costs were to be shared between the Norwegian government and the Israeli partner, the Andrea and Charles Bronfman Philanthropists. The moment when the programme was ready for launch coincided with the arrival in office of Israeli Prime Minister Binyamin Netanyahu, who made no secret of his negative views on the Oslo process. Consequently, just when the programme was operational, 'the political context completely changed its opportunity situation.'[7]

In the absence of further official encouragement for P2P the organisers gave up their institutional approach and went, as it were, 'freelance'. The programme also 'became "reactive" in the sense that it reacted to applications from others, rather than proactively defining interventions itself.'[8] Nonetheless, the authorities on both sides remained cooperative at least and the P2P initiatives did endure, that is, until February 2001 when 'The two peoples got engaged in hot conflict....and People-to-People activities became almost impossible to carry out.'[9]

Crucially, 'in the absence of a peace process, the critics of people-to-people projects got the upper hand' and an umbrella organisation for NGOs 'decided to expel the members who participated in such activities, criticising them for "collaborating" with the occupier, as well as being financed with foreign funds through Israeli organisations.'[10] Among Hanssen-Bauer's conclusions on 'what went wrong' he opined that 'unfortunately, the conflict was always present and controlled the structure of the encounters'; 'Israelis and Palestinians did not

---

[6] Hanssen-Bauer, J. (2005/6) 'Bustling Backwards: Lessons from the Norwegian Sponsored Israeli-Palestinian People-to-People Program' *Palestine-Israel Journal.* 12(4) & 13(1), p.39.

[7] Ibid., p.42.

[8] Ibid., p.42.

[9] Ibid., p.45.

[10] Ibid., pp.46-47.

meet as equals'; and:

> The Israeli organisations tend to be more experienced and professional in dealing with European and American donors. Thus, unwittingly and with the best intentions, they tended to become paternalistic and to reproduce the relations of dominance that prevailed in the political domain.[11]

Thus it was that, by the early 2000s, the local context for P2P dialogue between Israelis and Palestinians was doubly unconducive. The impetus to make a deal had broken down at the leadership level and there was active hostility to such exercises at the grassroots level.

The international context was equally unfavourable. The Clinton administration failed to broker peace, not least because it prioritised Israeli demands over those of the Palestinians.[12] When he came to power in January 2001, US President George W. Bush initially showed little interest in pursuing the MEPP and when the attacks on the World Trade Centre and the Pentagon occurred on 11 September 2001 he became preoccupied with the 'war on terror', the invasion of Afghanistan and thereafter Iraq.

When Bush did eventually articulate 'a vision' for peace – the 'two state solution' – in 2002, the EU latched on to this and within the Quartet (the UN, US, EU and Russia), Brussels took the lead in developing the Road Map designed to turn Bush's vision into a concrete plan. An exchange of letters between Israeli Prime Minister Ariel Sharon and President Bush accompanied the launch of the Road Map in 2003, rendering it more palatable to the Israelis and less so to the Palestinians, though both accepted it in principle. Yet neither demonstrated serious commitment to its implementation thereafter, including a provision for more grassroots dialogue exercises.

Investment in more P2P initiatives consequently devolved to the EU and was premised on the vain hope that the grassroots could be galvanised into the pursuit of peace despite their leaderships. In practice, activists on the Palestin-

---

[11] Ibid., p.48.

[12] See Miller, A. D. (2008) *The Much Too Promised Land: America's Elusive Search for Arab-Israeli Peace*. New York NY: Bantam Books; and Anziska, S. (2018) *Preventing Palestine: A Political History from Camp David to Oslo*. Princeton: Princeton University Press.

ian side generally shunned such activities as 'normalisation' i.e. accommodation to continued occupation, while belief in the value of P2P also waned on the Israeli side.

As will be discussed below, some activists on both sides subsequently turned their attention to campaigning in parallel for Palestinian rights. As their efforts demonstrated, for those committed to resolving the conflict the main focus shifted away from 'peace-building' through dialogue to raising awareness in Israel of the negative implications of continued occupation. That goal informs the design of the P2P exercises that are dedicated to 'conflict transformation' as opposed to 'window-dressing' and even these initiatives can only be transformative on a very limited scale, if at all, as explained below.

P2P and the Contact Hypothesis

Cross-conflict dialogue at the grassroots level may change the participants in a particular exercise, but it cannot transform society at large. To claim otherwise is to assume that when an individual changes his or her thinking, so will his or her community. Since this *cannot* be assumed, to generate change on a mass scale would require expanding the scope of P2P exercises to encompass most members of society. In the case of the Israelis and Palestinians only a small minority of each community has actually participated in cross-conflict dialogue and even then, in most cases, not on a sustained basis.

The theory that has informed most exercises in people-to-people dialogue is 'contact theory' and in particular 'the Contact Hypothesis' developed by Gordon Allport in the 1950s.[13] In his work Allport depicts competition for material resources between different cultural, sectarian and class groups as the norm, but singles out ethnic conflict as a particular problem, since the conflict is not only over tangible assets such as land and economic resources, but also over power, respect and/or social status. According to Allport, in ethnic conflict not only do members of competing groups hold negative stereotypes of 'the other', but their prejudices impair their capacity to entertain rational arguments or evidence to the contrary. The 'difference between ordinary prejudgements and prejudice' according to Allport, 'is that one can discuss and rectify a prejudgement with-

---

[13] Allport, G.W. (1954). *The Nature of Prejudice*. Reading, Mass.: Addison-Wesley, reprinted, with a new Introduction and Foreword, by Basic Books, the *25th Anniversary Edition*, in 1979.

out [the] emotional resistance' encountered when there is prejudice.[14] In other words, Allport locates the problem of prejudice in the emotional predispositions of individuals, which may, in turn, be attributable to their conditioning.

In seeking a way to remedy this problem, Allport recognises that *everyday* contact between different ethnic group members in the workplace, in shops and on public transport, will not in and of itself diminish prejudice. On the contrary, such contact may well reinforce prejudice and hostility. Even equal status contact, on a sustained basis, such as in desegregated schools in the United States, cannot be expected to reduce antipathy in *all* individuals.

However, the argument goes, through *managed* forms of contact or integration, it should be possible, statistically speaking, to produce a positive effect on *most* of those involved. Thus:

> Prejudice (unless deeply rooted in the character structure of the individual) may be reduced by equal status contact between majority and minority groups in pursuit of common goals. The effect is greatly enhanced if this contact is sanctioned by institutional supports (i.e. by law, custom or local atmosphere), and provided it is of a sort that leads to the perception of common interests and common humanity between members of the two groups.[15]

The appeal of reasoning along these lines to those in the business of 'peacebuilding' through people-to-people dialogue is obvious. However, advocates of such contacts tend to downplay the importance of the 'institutional supports' or official sanctioning that Allport calls for. In addition, they base their hopes on a statistical calculation that by changing some individuals they can generate a trend. This is to ignore the statistical fallacy at the heart of such reasoning.

As argued compellingly by H.D. Forbes,[16] the flaw in the Contact Hypothesis as commonly embraced is the assumption that what happens to individuals in a group exercise will have a ripple effect on society at large. However, it is a statistical fallacy to generalise from the individual to a community, from the participant in an exercise – who may indeed revise his or her ideas and learn to

---

[14] Allport (1954 & 1979) p.9.

[15] Allport (1954 & 1979) p.281.

[16] Forbes, H.D. (1997) *Ethnic Conflict: Commerce, Culture and the Contact Hypothesis.* New Haven and London: Yale University Press.

abandon his or her prejudices – to the attitudes of the ethnic group from which the participant comes.

In *The Nature of Prejudice*, Allport tended simply to extrapolate from the interpersonal level to the intergroup level, as if intergroup relations consisted of nothing more than interpersonal relations writ large. He traced prejudice and discrimination to the moral and intellectual shortcomings of individuals, and he looked to individual therapy in one form or another – including 'genuine acquaintances' among individuals from different groups – to cure the conflicts between groups.[17]

By contrast, Forbes contends, the problem of prejudice 'has much more to do with impersonal causes – the tides of history – than with the sins of individuals.'[18]

To pursue this point further, the capacity of an individual to separate themselves from their group identity is questionable, in the sense that individual and group identity are mutually constituted. Through positive interaction with 'the other' an individual may become more aware of the contrasting and mutually exclusive narratives of competing groups, but then he or she thereby faces difficult choices about how to reposition themselves in society.

In her work, Hélène Pfeil posits a remedy for those who would otherwise find themselves outcasts or rebels against their own communities and authorities. She proposes that participants and alumni of grassroots dialogue groups together 'create and sustain a common lifeworld' (a concept developed by the philosopher Jürgen Habermas), or create a 'shared background of understanding across the sides of the Israeli-Palestinian divide.'[19]

This is an ideal, the realisation of which requires more conducive circumstances than have prevailed in the Israeli-Palestinian context, especially since the Israeli government has shown an increasing propensity to penalise any NGO activities which challenge the official narrative. It also requires the organisers and funders of grassroots dialogue to encourage exploratory discussion

---

[17] Forbes (1997) p.201.

[18] Ibid.

[19] Pfeil, H. (2015). 'Understanding the Dynamics of Israeli-Palestinian Grassroots Dialogue Workshops: the Contribution of a Habermasian Approach', *International Journal of Politics, Culture and Society.* 28, p.130.

without stipulating preferred outcomes or objectives (on which more below and in Chapter 6). Yet, as Pfeil herself notes, most such exercises adopt a 'problem-solving approach'[20] and conflict transformation requires much more extensive work at the grassroots level.

Another advocate of P2P as a mechanism for tackling prejudice within society is clinical psychologist and journalist Judy Kuriansky. She claims: 'the contact hypothesis in social psychology proposes that working together is an effective way to break down barriers between in-groups and out-groups.'[21] This strongly implies that Kuriansky, while seeing the value of an approach which helps transform both individual and group thinking, has simply not considered the limitations of such an approach identified by Forbes. She says that the participants in P2P exercises are not willing 'to wait for political solutions: they want to live in coexistence and mutual respect now.' To reinforce her message she quotes Archbishop Desmond Tutu's inspirational words: 'I am because you are', and 'We need each other...I need you in order to be me'; and 'to forgive is not just for you, it is for me'.

Presumably, Tutu was talking about the moral salvation of the self to be found in truth and reconciliation, *post* a peace agreement. However, as discussed above, absent such an agreement and given the flaws in the Contact Hypothesis, Kuriansky's faith in what can be achieved through P2P seems naive. She is inspired by the good intentions of the organisers of P2P work and claims, rather unconvincingly, simply that she 'believes they are making a difference.'[22] What Kuriansky exemplifies is an attitude I have frequently encountered among advocates of grassroots dialogue who seem to think that young people, by their very youth, are able to identify with one another and build bridges in a way that their political leaders resist.

Yet, young or old, male or female, the participants in grassroots dialogue bring their experiences of real life (and death) into any meeting with 'the other' and, as discussed in the next section, they are more invested in exercises which

---

[20] In her article Pfeil uses the term 'track two diplomacy' to refer to grassroots dialogue, which indicates that she shares the confusion of many, about the difference between Track II Diplomacy and P2P dialogue exercises. The job of Track II *is* to focus on discerning what it would take to make a deal – but that is not a viable approach in P2P exercises, as elucidated previously.

[21] Kuriansky, J. ed. (2007) *Beyond Bombs & Bullets: Grassroots Peacebuilding between Israelis and Palestinians*. Westpoint, Connecticut & London: Praeger, p.xxvi.

[22] Ibid.

confront those realities than those which downplay or avoid talking about them. The terms of engagement matter and a simple appeal to the common humanity of the individuals engaged in dialogue is likely to be received as a strategy for avoiding confronting difference.

Recognising Inequalities

As a number of studies have shown,[23] hitherto most P2P dialogue exercises involving Israelis and Palestinians have been based on the Contact Hypothesis. As even its originator Gordon Allport concedes, however, the terms on which individuals participate in group activities are vitally important. Allport advises that conditions of equality need to be created. The problem is that where some of the participants hail from the dominant group in society at large, and the others from disadvantaged or subordinate communities in the societal structure, it is impossible to proceed *as if* individual participants can forget their experiences of unequal status for the duration of the exercise.

According to researcher Ifat Maoz,[24] P2P exercises involving Israelis and Palestinians can be categorised into four main types, depending on their approach to dialogue. These are: (1) those based on the Coexistence Model, where the emphasis is on interpersonal similarities and cultural and language commonalities in order to promote 'mutual understanding', while avoiding discussions about national identity and Palestinian experiences of discrimination. Maoz has found this to be the dominant model guiding P2P activities. (2) The Joint Projects Model, 'based on the assumption that working together towards a common, superordinate goal reduces intergroup hostilities, increases liking and cooperation, and fosters a common identity transcending the separate identity of each group'. (3) The Confrontational Model, also called the Group Identity Model, wherein the participants discuss the conflict, their respective group roles in it and the power relations between them, to better understand identity con-

---

[23] See in particular Maoz, I. (2011) 'Does contact work in protracted asymmetrical conflict? Appraising 20 years of reconciliation-aimed encounters between Israeli Jews and Palestinians'. *Journal of Peace Research.* 48(1); and 'People-to-People: What Went Wrong and How to Fix It' (2005-06) *Palestine-Israel Journal.* 12(4) & 13(1).

[24] Maoz, I. (2011) 'Does contact work in protracted asymmetrical conflict? Appraising 20 years of reconciliation-aimed encounters between Israeli Jews and Palestinians'. *Journal of Peace Research.* 48(1).

struction and develop Israeli awareness of the asymmetries. (4) The Narrative Model, which combines the coexistence and confrontation aspects and understandings of the conflict. Based on work by social-psychologists Dan Bar-On and Sami Adwan, this last model uses a narrative approach in which the participants engage in story-telling about their lives.

Using this taxonomy, Maoz identifies the positive potential of each approach, but also reveals the problems each entail. Model (1) can lead to disappointment and alienation, and effectively perpetuates the asymmetrical power relations, by concentrating on 'changing individual-level prejudice while ignoring the need to address collective and institutionalised bases of discrimination.'[25] Model (2) can also lead to frustration since it does not address directly the power relations which prevail outside the exercise and these can become manifest within it. Model (3) can 'distress and alienate Jewish participants and cause negative attitudes and distrust towards Arabs and towards the practice of encounters.'[26] Model (4) also has limitations in so far as the participants face an impossible task of combining the personal with the collective, the factual with the emotional, in the choice and delivery of their stories.

The value of Maoz's work for would-be organisers of P2P exercises is clearly in pointing out the pitfalls of the various approaches that have been adopted to date. Also, she does not fall into the trap identified by Forbes of expecting societal transformation as a result of P2P workshops. Her findings are substantiated in the reports of a number of P2P participants who contributed to a special issue of the *Palestine-Israel Journal* (2005-06) that explored 'what went wrong' with People-to-People dialogue exercises from 1995 to 2006.

According to Nadia Nasser-Najjab, while Palestinians typically entered a P2P exercise seeking to reveal to their Israeli counterparts the extent of their suffering under the occupation, the Israelis arrived with an assumption that the Oslo process constituted the solution to the Palestinian problem. As she puts it:

Israelis were more concerned about future relations between Palestinians and Israelis and did not want to hear about conflict and the political aspects because this was too painful and already in the past. But what was history

---

[25] Ibid., p.118.

[26] Ibid., p.120.

for Israelis was the future for Palestinians.[27]

Palestinians also experienced difficulties travelling to meetings with Israelis because of the closures imposed on the West Bank that prevented Palestinians accessing East Jerusalem even before the security barrier was erected.[28] They would arrive late, distressed and resentful that their Israeli counterparts suffered no such indignities or impediments to movement. When they met overseas their passage out to such meetings via Ben Gurion airport would be facilitated by their Israeli partners, compounding their sense of inequality.

Lack of follow-up to joint ventures in their respective communities was also a problem. In their introduction to the Journal, Nasser-Najjab and Lee Perlman say: 'contact between Palestinians and Israelis appeared to fail to produce any meaningful influence on the attitudes of the participants within and beyond the timeframe of the meetings'.[29] According to Salim Tamari, another contributor to the Journal, the sponsors of P2P dictated not only the themes to be addressed, but often also required inclusion of both Israelis and Palestinians in the activities, thereby ruling out some capacity-building initiatives that might have been better pursued in separate groups. Tamari also said that the sponsors preferred projects which promised to build understanding, but not those that promised to rectify the root problem of the occupation.

Prioritising Group Identities

In contrast to most of the P2P exercises based on the Contact Hypothesis and/or that attempted to downplay or circumvent the imbalance in power that frames Israeli-Palestinian relations, one organisation has sought to focus on the differences that distinguish Israelis and Palestinians. This is the School for Peace, based at the shared Israeli-Palestinian village of Wahat as-Salam/Neve Shalom (Oasis of Peace) set up in 1972.[30]

---

[27] Nasser-Najjab, N. 'Post-Oslo Dialogue: An Evaluation' in 'People-to-People: What Went Wrong and How to Fix It' (2005-06) *Palestine-Israel Journal*. 12(4) & 13(1), p.31.

[28] For more on this factor see Chapter 5.

[29] 'People-to-People: What Went Wrong and How to Fix It' (2005-06) *Palestine-Israel Journal*. 12(4) & 13(1), p.6.

[30] See Rabah Halabi, ed. *Israeli and Palestinian Identities in Dialogue: The School for Peace Approach* first published in Hebrew in 2000, the English translation of which appeared in 2004; and Liat Tuv, *Talking through Difference: Everyday Ethics Across Borders in an Israeli-Palestinian Community*, unpublished PhD Thesis, LSE January 2018.

In complete contrast to the methodologies used in most P2P exercises, the School for Peace, through its work over many years, developed a model for cross-conflict dialogue which tackled directly the inequalities and asymmetries that frame real life relations between the Israelis and Palestinians.

> We understood that stereotypes are only the visible, superficial symptom and that, as such, they can reveal the much deeper underlying conceptions held by both Jews and Arabs. These ideas are hard to eradicate: they are formed by the conflict and also reinforce it. We came to see that cordial contact ('eating hummus together'), may provide a good feeling for the moment but solves nothing, rather it helps preserve the status quo and even fortifies it.[31]

Through trial and error, the School for Peace created an approach which deliberately encouraged the examination, reconstruction and consolidation of the two group identities 'because only an encounter between confident identities can lead to a genuine meeting of equals and permit the option of building a more humane and just society.'[32]

It is important to note, however, that in their book about the School for Peace approach, Rabah Halabi and his colleagues described their work with Palestinian and Jewish *citizens of Israel*, rather than mediation between Israelis and the Palestinians living under occupation in the West Bank and Gaza Strip. The parameters are different, in that, inside Israel the Jews are the majority and the Palestinians the minority, and both hold citizenship. In that context, Halabi and his colleagues saw their task as enabling Jewish and Palestinian citizens of Israel to accept their separate group identities, not pretend they are all the same, and *thence* confront the realities of their inequality:

> These meetings cannot, and are not intended to, change reality. What they can and do change is the participants' awareness of the conflict and their

---

[31] Halabi, R. (2004) *Israeli and Palestinian Identities in Dialogue: The School for Peace Approach* New Brunswick, New Jersey and London: Rutgers University Press, p.28.

[32] Ibid.

social and political identity.[33]

In the process, according to Halabi and colleagues, the Palestinians can gain a sense of solidarity and agency – at least for the duration of the encounter – while the Jews likely become angry as they begin to see that acknowledgement of their own position of superiority and their oppression of 'the other' brings into question the legitimacy of their very presence and position. The hope was that:

> Taking responsibility in the Jewish group for racism or power or discrimination rehabilitates to a great extent the group's damaged national identity and builds a more positive and healthier one.[34]

As should be apparent, such encounter exercises are fraught with tensions and can be very uncomfortable for the participants, especially Jewish Israelis. Certainly, this was what I observed in the encounters which I co-facilitated. The Palestinian participants obliged their Jewish Israeli counterparts to listen to their stories of life under occupation (or the blockade, in the case of Gaza) and refused to excuse what for them was so blatantly unfair about their situation – causing the Jewish Israelis to face up to the asymmetry of the relationship between themselves and the Palestinians as a people. There is much more on this subject in subsequent chapters, in particular Chapters 5 and 6.

In conclusion here, as will no doubt be apparent, the insights of Halabi and his colleagues give little solace to those who wish to depict P2P activities as conducive to peace-making between communities, at least not in the near term. Instead, according to the School for Peace model, such exercises must acknowledge the reality of the occupation, confront it and then spread the word that only by ending the occupation can peace be attained. In view of this, it should be no surprise that the political leadership on the Israeli side has become more hostile to grassroots activists who wish to do just that and rail against the Euro-

---

[33] Halabi and Nava Sonnenschein, 'Awareness, Identity and Reality' in Halabi, ed. (2004) *Israeli and Palestinian Identities in Dialogue: The School for Peace Approach.* p.54.

[34] Sonnenschein and Ahmad Hijazi "'Home Group" the Uninational Framework' in Halabi, ed. (2004) *Israeli and Palestinian Identities in Dialogue: The School for Peace Approach.* p.174.

peans for funding activities that appear to 'delegitimise' Israel.[35]

In the next chapter the discussion shifts to a description of the composition, terms of engagement and goals of the cross-conflict exercise that I co-facilitated for eight years. This will set the scene for subsequent chapters in which I explore the findings we made about the role of national narratives in driving conflict.

---

[35] In March 2019 the School for Peace issued an urgent appeal for donations, having been informed that the US Government was cancelling its $1million grant to the School as part of the US administration's decision to cease all USAID funding to Palestinian recipients.

2
Talking to the Enemy –
Mechanics and Dynamics

By talking to the enemy face-to-face the protagonists in a conflict can find themselves on a fascinating path of discovery, provided the parameters of the encounter have been carefully thought through in advance. For the participants, the experience will very likely challenge some of their most cherished and/or unacknowledged beliefs about their opponents *and* themselves. It is not, therefore, an undertaking to be entered lightly or sampled briefly, only to quit when the encounter proves disorientating.

There is, however, no learning without dissonance.[1] The value of cross-conflict dialogue lies above all, I contend, in its potential to deepen understanding of 'self and other' and thence learn more about the drivers and dynamics of conflict than is possible without such contact or some other type of challenge to insular thinking.[2]

I am talking here about the potential of cross-conflict dialogue explicitly as an exploratory exercise, not as a process by which the participants intend to negotiate an agreement. As discussed in the previous chapter, *negotiations* are the business of political leaders and officials, and not to be confused with so-called 'people-to-people' (P2P) encounters. When the latter are burdened with expectations that success means reaching agreement, the participants are deprived of an opportunity to simply explore and reflect for its own sake. Unrealistic expectations will also set them up for failure. [3]

In order for a dialogue exercise to maximize the potential for participant learning, it is also necessary to be attentive to the broader context. When that

---

[1] On which more later in this chapter.

[2] For example, spending time in a society or culture different to that in which one initially grew up.

[3] Marco Pinfari writes discerningly about the wishful thinking that very often drives well-meaning initiatives of this sort. See Pinfari. M. (2005) 'Conservative Counter-Reformation or Disillusionment: Reply to Michel Warschawski' *Rutgers Student Journal of Israeli Affairs*, pp.16-17.

is not conducive, P2P dialogue is a potentially hazardous undertaking for both the participants and the organisers. The latter need to protect the exercise from external interference or sabotage, *and* they must 'hold' the group through the difficult process of learning.

What I mean by this will become clear shortly, but for now suffice to say that when ordinary members of society, as opposed to officials, talk to the enemy, they will face scepticism and hostility from those not so engaged. This is in part because, even when political leaders say they want peace, yet blame the other side for its absence, they may be indicating that continuation of the status quo suits them better than its transformation. After all, demonising and dehumanising an enemy makes it easier to justify or tolerate the use of violence against them. Also, so long as the enemy can be portrayed as implacable and irredeemable, it can be held responsible for this or that problem and used as a scapegoat.

There will always be those who prefer to avoid discovering, through engagement, that the enemy is quite unlike the monster they have heard about[4] or that their own narrative warrants re-examination. Also, in so far as they might develop greater understanding of 'the other', those who dare to talk to the enemy could find themselves accused of breaking ranks, treachery even, on their own side. To protect themselves from such charges, participants may duck the learning opportunity and instead use the encounter to vent their hostility and thereby simply pursue the conflict by other means.

Consequently, it is the responsibility of the organisers of dialogue to provide some protection for those with the curiosity to want to explore. This means, in so far as possible, ensuring that the proceedings remain confidential and away from the glare of publicity. It also means that, from the beginning, the participants need to be given a definition of success which does not include reaching agreement with one another, but which does mean using the opportunity to listen as well as speak.

Beyond these basics, several other considerations have to be factored into the planning. There has to be some incentive to stay with the dialogue when the going gets tough. Curiosity about 'the other' is a necessary basis for participant engagement and at the very least, it can incline participants to listen as well as speak. Yet it will not be enough to sustain the endeavour when anger and dis-

---

[4] Pinfari, M. (2018) *Terrorists as Monsters*. Oxford: Oxford University Press.

tress become manifest.

As I have learned, a key benefit that dialogue participants can derive from their encounter is a greater sense of their own individual agency, including the capacity to manage their emotions and to weigh their options before choosing a course of action, especially in the face of provocation. The way I have explained what I mean here is to invite a person to envisage a glass divide between themselves and an interlocutor toward whom or from whom they experience hostility. The glass is a metaphor for the mental shield they can erect to give themselves time and space to consider their options. That is, a kind of pause for thought, to ponder the utility of jumping to action – shouting an insult or slinging a punch – versus holding fire. To the extent possible, the dictum to 'choose your battles' is worth heeding.

Even so, at the beginning of a dialogue exercise, the concept of developing greater personal agency will probably not have much resonance for participants. Much more compelling, in my experience, is the promise of something more tangible or substantive, such as attaining new skills, or qualifications. Also, progress toward acquiring these benefits needs to be palpable, as explained below.

Other factors which require consideration in the design of a dialogue exercise include the size of the group engaged in the endeavour – if it is too big, some of those present will simply allow others to do the heavy lifting and become bystanders. If it is too small the potential for learning through working with intragroup dynamics and sub-group identities is absent. The demographics of the group – age, nationality, gender balance, geographical derivation – will affect the scope and tenor of the discussion. The location of the meetings – type of venue, its accessibility and provisions for security – will determine the level of engagement of participants. The ground rules established for the exercise and the credentials and approach of facilitators are also of crucial importance to what can be accomplished.

In the remainder of this chapter I shall explain how all these issues were handled in the case of the cross-conflict dialogue exercise that I co-facilitated and which led me to make the observations and discoveries that form the basis of this book. After setting the scene here, those findings are explored in subsequent chapters.

An Educational Framework

My experience with P2P derives from a most unusual, probably unique, exercise which contrasts with all the other initiatives of which I am aware. That is because, what was on offer to participants in the Olive Tree Programme that I took over and reconfigured at City, University of London, from 2008 to 2016 was not only or even primarily an opportunity to 'talk to the enemy'. The core offer was a full scholarship to study for an undergraduate degree, in any of the disciplines taught at City. The chance of gaining such a scholarship, inclusive of the full cost of overseas student fees, a bursary and international travel expenses, for three years, was the primary motivation for all those who applied.

For sure the applicants understood that attainment of one of the Olive Tree scholarships would also entail participation in a parallel programme of cross-conflict dialogue during the three years that it would take them to gain their degree. For some of the successful applicants, particularly though not exclusively, the Israelis, this component of 'the offer' was an added attraction. For others, especially in the case of some Palestinians, this aspect of the Olive Tree Programme was a potential hazard or detraction, but not such as to deter them from applying. All those successful applicants who had reservations but took up their scholarships saw the benefits of gaining a degree at a university in London – something almost all of them could not have afforded otherwise – as sufficiently attractive to outweigh their misgivings.

To reinforce this claim, I can attest that not all the applicants offered a scholarship under the Olive Tree Programme took up their awards. One such Israeli applicant professed that she had already experienced her fill of cross-conflict dialogue. In this, she was exceptional. Another applicant explained that his parents could afford to send him to America to study and that attracted him more than the Olive Tree offer. Two successful Palestinian applicants decided to decline their scholarships, based on several considerations including family and peer pressure, plus the fact that they were already half-way through undergraduate degree programmes elsewhere – one in Cyprus, the other in Ramallah.

There were, however, a few successful Israeli applicants who chose to abandon degree courses in Tel Aviv in order to start afresh at City. A number of Palestinians also either left off their studies in Gaza or the West Bank to begin again in London or, having already actually completed one degree at a local university, nonetheless wanted another degree from a more prestigious university. In addition, the chance of escaping the perils and confinement of life in the Gaza Strip was a big pull for all the Gazan Palestinians accepted onto the Programme. The majority of them subsequently found ways to remain abroad, thereby advancing in their chosen professions in ways that they could not possibly have achieved 'back home'. All of them also treated it as a matter of course that they would work to give financial support to the families they left behind.

The fact that the Olive Tree was first and foremost a scholarship programme, as opposed to simply a P2P exercise, had incalculable significance for the selection and retention of participants. To be considered for a scholarship every applicant had to meet the criteria for access to their preferred degree programme at City, which varied depending on the discipline concerned. They all had to attain a specified minimum score in a standard English language test and the required grades in subjects relevant to their chosen degree programme.

During the period in which I directed the Olive Tree Programme, the bar (or 'tariff' as it is called) for Palestinian applicants to British universities was raised to include specified grades in at least one year of studies at an officially approved university, or proof of one year's work experience. By contrast, adequate scores in their final year of secondary school were deemed sufficient for Israeli applicants, on the grounds that the calibre of secondary education in Israel, but not necessarily in the West Bank and Gaza, is on a par with that in British secondary schools. In recent years also, the British government has standardised the requirements for an overseas student visa and made British universities responsible for making sure those requirements are met.

As a result of university requirements for entry and government visa regulations, therefore, the pool of qualified candidates for Olive Tree scholarships was much smaller than the total number of initial applicants. Between 2008 and 2016, there were three rounds of scholarships on offer (in 2008, 2010 and 2013) and in each case half the scholarships were allocated for Israelis and half for Palestinians.[5] The total number of Israeli citizens awarded scholarships represented about a third of those who met the requirements. In the case of the Palestinians from Gaza and the West Bank, those accepted constituted roughly three-quarters of those who met all the formal requirements for entry.

The explanation for these contrasting figures can be attributed to the different socio-economic circumstances of the applicants. They also highlight one of the reasons why the Olive Tree could not be easily replicated on a large scale – since the pool of qualified applicants, particularly Palestinians, was so

[5] In each cohort there were also one or two Palestinians holding Israeli citizenship and passports.

small. On average, the Israelis had more access to higher quality secondary and tertiary level education than the Palestinians. Each Israeli had also had more opportunities to travel internationally than the average Palestinian. That said, virtually none of either group could have afforded three years' study at a London university without a scholarship and they had this in common with each other. They entered the Programme on an equal basis in terms of academic merit. In this respect also, both the Israelis and the Palestinians accepted onto the Olive Tree Programme came from a relatively exceptional minority in their respective societies.

In order to determine which of the qualified applicants would be awarded scholarships, the selection process involved first the evaluation of their written applications and then interviews. Each applicant also had to provide the names of two referees, from whom references were sought in the event that a candidate made it through to the interview stage. In their written applications candidates had to provide a 'personal statement' explaining (a) Why you want to be an Olive Tree scholar? (b) What will the programme mean to you? (c) How do you think the programme will challenge you? and (d) How do you think you will contribute to the programme? They were also requested to list their work experience and/or voluntary/community activities.

For the duration of my time as director of Olive Tree I was able to employ one or two part-time assistants drawn from among the alumni of the Programme, both Israeli and Palestinian. These individuals made themselves available, by e-mail and phone, to answer applicant questions and would communicate in their native language or English as appropriate. Thanks to them, the applicants were reassured that there were no predetermined or ideal answers to the questions, but rather, what was wanted was a demonstration that they had given thought to what might be involved and what it would mean for them. I also had the help of a colleague, my co-facilitator, in evaluating the written applications.

When it came to the interviews, I was assisted by two colleagues, one of them my co-facilitator and the other either an Israeli academic or a Palestinian academic, depending on the nationality of the interviewee. These academics were individuals known to me from my previous work in the field. The interviews were conducted in English and in almost all cases Israeli citizens were interviewed in Tel Aviv and the Palestinians in Ramallah or by video-link to Gaza. My colleagues and I followed an agreed procedure in the interviews, taking it in turns to ask different questions, but always following the same basic format with each candidate. The Israeli academic participated in shortlisting the Israeli candidates and the Palestinian in short-listing the Palestinian candidates.

Group Demographics

In total there were five cohorts of Olive Tree scholarship students, two of them recruited before I became director in 2008. By 2008 the first Olive Tree cohort had already graduated and the second cohort were in the second year of their degree programmes. The composition of each cohort, in terms of the gender balance and derivation of the participants, varied across the cohorts, as summarised here:

Cohort	Male	Female
1 2004-7	6 Jewish Israelis 2 Palestinians from East Jerusalem 2 West Bank Palestinians 4 Gazan Palestinians	1 Jewish Israeli 1 Palestinian Israeli
2 2006-9	3 Jewish Israelis (2 of whom were from settlements in the West Bank) 1 Palestinian Israeli 2 West Bank Palestinians 2 Gazan Palestinians	2 Jewish Israelis 2 Palestinians from East Jerusalem

3 2008-11	3 Jewish Israelis 2 West Bank Palestinians (1 of-whom dropped out after 1 year)	2 Jewish Israelis 2 Gazan Palestinians 2 West Bank Palestinians 1 Palestinian Israeli
4 2009-12	2 Jewish Israelis 1 West Bank Palestinian 1 Gazan Palestinian	2 Jewish Israelis 2 Palestinian Israelis 1 West Bank Palestinian
5 2013-16	2 Jewish Israelis 1 Palestinian from East Jerusalem 1 West Bank Palestinian 2 Gazan Palestinians	2 Jewish Israelis 2 Palestinian Israelis

There was considerable diversity in the range of disciplines that the scholars chose to study. The most popular degree choice of the Palestinian men of the first and second cohorts was either Engineering or Journalism, though in subsequent cohorts their choices also included International Politics and Sociology. Two of the Palestinian women opted to study Business, one the Law, one Biomedical Engineering, two Psychology and two International Politics. Of the Jewish Israelis, male or female, the majority opted to study for Social Science degrees (International Politics, Sociology, Psychology and Journalism), one chose Business, another Engineering and one the Law.

Various factors influenced the choices made. Those Palestinians, as well as the Israeli, who chose to study Engineering – in most cases some aspect of Computer Programming and IT – reported cultural norms and family pressure as instrumental in their decision to go for a discipline that would enhance their employment prospects. Those who chose to study Journalism also saw this as a route to future employment in a respected profession. Similar calculations, along with aptitude, influenced those who chose to study Law, Business and

Psychology. By contrast, those who opted to undertake degrees in International Politics and Sociology saw themselves as on a quest to better understand the world around them.

As will be apparent, there was a more even gender balance in the third, fourth and fifth cohorts than in the first two. Since I only became director of the Programme after the members of the first cohort had graduated, I was not able to form an opinion on how the predominance of males in that group affected the dynamics of intra-group relations and discussions. Also, I am reluctant to attribute too much weight to the significance of gender balance given that there were so many other factors at work, in particular national identity and the effect on the students of developments in the Israeli-Palestinian conflict 'back home', on which there will be much more to say in due course. Suffice to say, though, that I did notice a contrast in the styles of interaction when women slightly outnumbered the men, as in the third and fourth cohorts, compared to when men predominated, as in the second and fifth cohorts. In the latter instances the dynamic was more overtly volatile, and the language could be more threatening. In all cases, however, the women were no less assertive and capable of expressing strong views than the men.

The ages of the participants when they entered the programme was be-tween nineteen and twenty-six. Almost all of the Jewish Israelis had completed at least two or three years of military service, some in combat units, some in 'Intelligence', before applying for a scholarship. As a result, the average age of the Israelis was slightly older than that of the Palestinians. All the participants had had a lifetime of experiencing – living in – the conflict and exposure to violence to varying extents. Some, on both sides, had suffered trauma and had some level of post-traumatic stress to deal with. Most had lost someone close to them as a result of the conflict. A number had suffered injury or knew well someone who had.

In many respects, therefore, the Olive Tree scholars had attained a level of maturity and experience (some of it extremely testing[6]) that contrasted with the broader undergraduate population at City, though the demographic of under-graduates at City is more diverse than at most British universities and includes many first-generation migrants of various ethnic and religious backgrounds. In many respects, the Olive Tree scholars were keen to identify with the rest of the

---

[6] On which more shortly and in Chapter 5.

student body and experience student life accordingly, inclusive of developing friendships with fellow students in their degree programmes and in the residence halls, where all of them were housed for at least their first year. At least three of the scholars were already married before coming to London and were joined by their spouses after the first year. Some scholars formed relationships within the programme and one couple subsequently married, though I am not aware of any partnerships between an Israeli and a Palestinian.

As will be apparent, it is impossible to compare the Olive Tree experience with the P2P exercises undertaken in the region. The chance of studying in London and enrolment at City was what brought the participants together. Without that incentive, I contend, it is essentially inconceivable that successive groups of talented and ambitious Israelis and Palestinians could have been enjoined to sustain an intensive dialogue with each other over a full three-year period. Crucially also, they did this in London, thousands of miles away from their homes, their societies and the conflict. They were all, in effect, obliged to stick with the dialogue exercise, as the price for retaining their scholarships.

When accepting their scholarships I required the students to confirm their commitment to:

• Fulfil the requirements of their academic degree programme, including attending classes, completing assignments and sitting exams; and

• Attend all the Olive Tree Scholarship Programme meetings and activities, including Wednesday afternoon sessions during term time, field trips and the annual excursion.

They were also required to fill out evaluations and/or questionnaires about their experience, year by year, most of which were done anonymously. The format of these varied for each cohort, about which more later. The main point though is that continuance of their scholarship depended not only on attending to their studies but also showing up for the dialogue sessions. Of the fifty-nine applicants accepted onto the programme over twelve years only one dropped out and that person did so as a result of failing to meet the academic requirements for progression.

The Venue and Setting

The setting in which the dialogue took place, that is an institution of higher education in a 'third country', outside the conflict zone, was important in several respects. Notably, the participating students found themselves in a multi-cultural, multi-ethnic and multi-sectarian setting where they were all on a par with, and in amongst, thousands of other students. Both the Israelis and the Palestinians were in a sense thereby liberated from the asymmetric relations that define their dealings with one another 'back home'. Like all the other students at the university, they were graded, and their progress rated, purely on the basis of their academic performance.

The language of instruction at City being English, all the Israelis and Palestinians had to become fluent in English and their knowledge of either Hebrew or Arabic afforded them no advantage. Even though some of the students arrived speaking better English than others, it was not the case that this reflected national differences. On both sides there was considerable variation in the level of English spoken initially and individually they all gained greater facility over time. This development proved empowering and affirming for each of them.

Crucially also, a university is designed to impart and encourage learning and intellectual growth. By tradition in Britain, though arguably less so these days, the ethos of higher education is to challenge students to explore, discover, question, experiment, examine, analyse and debate as well as research and extend their knowledge and understanding. Thus, the setting in which this particular cross-conflict dialogue took place was conducive for learning in general and experimenting with new ideas in particular. It is hard to imagine that the participants in the programme would have been as adventurous and 'open' as they proved to be, had they been persuaded to meet in a different setting, especially one located in the conflict zone and on the home territory of one or other of the parties.

This point deserves further emphasis. As educational psychologists will attest, there is no learning without dissonance. In other words, intellectual growth is less an incremental or linear process than it is a series of leaps from one level of understanding and insight to another. As described by Thomas Kuhn in his book *The Structure of Scientific Revolutions*,[7] each significant advance in scientific theory is preceded by a period of struggle during which the researcher attempts to make his or her observations conform to the expectations of existing theories, before finally making a mental leap to a new way of understanding what those observations might mean. Consequently, learning requires letting go of hitherto cherished and seemingly self-affirming ways of viewing the world to make

---

[7] Kuhn, T. S. (1970) *The Structure of Scientific Revolutions*. Chicago University Press.

possible the embrace of a new way of understanding.

William Perry's schema for making sense of the progression that university students can be expected to experience is helpful here.[8] As he describes it, as children we are taught to distinguish between right and wrong and to apply this distinction to learn the right answers to questions. We are unsettled when we discover that some questions cannot be answered by acquiring more information. Instead we become baffled and irritated when the discovery of more 'facts' does not establish who or what is right and who or what is wrong. Faced with complexity, we may either walk away from the problem, 'drop out' even, or else embrace a relativist outlook, that allows for a range of perspectives to co-exist among which we may choose according to our preference.

According to Perry, the goal is to enable students to move from 'dualism' to 'relativism', but not to stop at that point. Rather, students should be encouraged to discover how the tools of different disciplines can lead us to different conclusions and the validity of these will depend on which theoretical and/or philosophical frameworks we apply. Awareness and explicit acknowledgement of how we validate our discoveries then becomes a new way of seeing and understanding through which each of us can manage our encounters with complexity, accept diversity and make considered choices.

I was introduced to Perry's theories when I first started teaching undergraduates at George Washington University in Washington, D.C. in the 1980s. I wanted to learn about the ethos of higher education, the better to understand my responsibilities as an instructor. Amongst academic colleagues at City I did not discover any who were consciously aware of Perry's work, but there were many who understood and agreed with the general thrust of his thinking on how learning takes place and needs to be encouraged. In particular, the view prevails that students learn most when they are supported to grapple with complex questions, read widely, debate and make their own discoveries, as opposed to simply listening to lectures, taking notes and regurgitating what they have heard or read in their exams and papers.

In any case, the insights of Kuhn and Perry, together with the dictum that 'there is no learning without dissonance,' informed the way I set about designing and facilitating the dialogue between Israelis and Palestinians enrolled in the Olive Tree Programme.

---

[8] See https://cse.buffalo.edu/~rapaport/perry.positions.html

Facilitation and Infrastructure

During my time as director of the Olive Tree, facilitation of dialogue sessions was almost always done by two people working as a team, and almost always one man and one woman with relevant experience and expertise. The normal practice in the various P2P exercises run by organisations in the region is for facilitation to be provided by one Jew and one Arab working in tandem. I am neither Jewish nor Arab, but I did have the benefit of years of research on the Israeli-Palestinian conflict (among others), many personal and professional contacts and friends on both sides, and years of experience facilitating and participating in so-called Track II exercises (see Chapter 1).

I had three co-facilitators during my years with the Olive Tree. First Sam McBratney (from 2008 to 2013) plus, over four years, Nick Townsend, a colleague from the 'Academic Learning Support' team at City, and then Damian Gorman (from 2013 to 2016). Nick also supported some of the students individually in a manner available to all City students seeking help with completing their assignments on time. Sam is a Methodist Minister, originally from Northern Ireland, who combined his role with Olive Tree with that of University Chaplain at City.

After Sam left City in 2013, he was replaced by Damian who had already become familiar with the Olive Tree by facilitating sessions with successive cohorts when they visited the Corrymeela Community centres in Ballycastle and Belfast for residential retreats at the end of the summer term. Damian is an Irish playwright and poet and had accumulated years of experience in cross-conflict dialogue in the Irish as well as other contexts, including the Balkans. Both Sam and Damian have spent time on the ground in the Israeli-Palestinian context and both brought to the Olive Tree dialogue different sets of skills and experience which, I believe, contrasted with and complimented my own.

The dialogue sessions took place every Wednesday afternoon, at City, during term time. At the beginning of the Autumn and Spring terms we would also have a weekend 'retreat' with the students, run by one or two of the staff from Corrymeela and, in most cases Damian. At the end of the summer term it was our usual practice to take the students to Corrymeela or a venue in the Republic of Ireland, in one case to the Netherlands, and a couple of times to a retreat in the Oxfordshire countryside, for a five-day residential retreat.

The main purpose of taking the students to Ireland, particularly Northern Ireland, was to give them a chance to meet and learn from activists, former members of paramilitary groups and others with stories to tell about their experiences during 'The Troubles' in Northern Ireland. It was thanks to the experienced staff who worked for Corrymeela, initially Ronnie Miller and then Susan McEwen in particular, that successive cohorts of Olive Tree students were able to participate in the type of interactions and activities for which the Corrymeela Community is well known and respected in Northern Ireland.

When we took the fifth cohort to the Netherlands in 2015 the intention was to enable them to learn about how the Dutch were handling the challenges posed by ethnic and sectarian diversity in their increasingly multicultural society. In all cases the residential retreats provided a change of scene and opportunity to explore issues and converse, interspersed with visits to sites of interest, relaxation and outdoor pursuits.

Throughout my time with Olive Tree, I, my co-facilitators, and the students, had the benefit of support from members of the professional staff at City, in particular Andrea Kenneally (Head of Neurodiversity, Disability and Academic Learning Support) and Charlotte Halvorsen (Head of the Student Counselling Service). Andrea and Charlotte were available to all the students for individual consultation and mentoring. Charlotte also convened weekly meetings at which the Olive Tree staff team could discuss pressing issues and concerns, coordinate responses and ensure 'best practice'. Reflecting on their involvement, Charlotte and Andrea said:

> The opportunity to work on this programme, with both the other staff and the students, was not without its challenges as we faced a complex task. However, the bringing together of our expertise in providing support to them, within an educational context, together with much reflection and thought being integrated into the process, encouraged learning to take place for us all. It was a privilege to work with such dedicated colleagues and inspirational students, with much unknown as we found the way to best understand what had been undertaken by us all.

Given their expertise and experience with university students living away from home for the first time, many of them coming from difficult social and family backgrounds, Charlotte and Andrea were acutely aware of the complex issues faced in particular by the Olive Tree scholars. They had to grapple with the challenges typically faced by young adults at the same time as being expected to 'talk to the enemy' along the way. It was therefore thanks to Charlotte and Andrea that the scholars were ensured the support and understanding essential to providing for their basic care.

For my part, not only could I look to them for advice, but I also had guidance from my line-manager, City's Deputy Vice-Chancellor (International), Professor Dinos Arcoumanis. To my great good fortune, he backed me absolutely in reconfiguring the Olive Tree to focus on the academic and learning opportunities it afforded to the scholars, as opposed to treating it as another facet of what I choose to call the 'peace business' (discussed in Chapters 1 and 6).

At Charlotte Halvorsen's instigation, I also had the benefit of a monthly consultation with a very wise and inspirational mentor, Dr Anton Obholzer – a consultant psychiatrist and psychoanalyst, and former Chief Executive of the Tavistock Centre. In addition to guiding and encouraging me, Anton also ran some workshops for the Olive Tree staff team and met the students in each cohort for at least one discussion during their time at the university. Anton helped me better understand and resolve many of the dilemmas I faced as director of Olive Tree and aided me in formulating my discoveries and insights.

Last but not least, I and the Programme benefitted from the goodwill and technical support of many of the staff at City who assisted us with the day-to-day running of the programme, including the admission and visa processes and accounts. The technical support team of the Journalism Department also helped us with the audio-visuals for the series of panel discussions, with visiting speakers (branded the Olive Tree Middle East Forum) which I devised as a way of reaching out to the whole student body and providing Olive Tree with a public profile. Attendees included members of the public who were supportive of Olive Tree. As many of the university staff explained to me, for them Olive Tree represented an inspiration and commitment, over and above the usual business of a university, that they valued.

I have indulged in this amount of detail about the staffing and support-base of the programme for three reasons. First, in order to convey that the Olive Tree was very much a team effort and the beneficiary of a very knowledgeable and experienced team at that. Second, the sheer infrastructural magnitude and related cost of the whole endeavour needs understanding to appreciate the significance of the findings that it has yielded, and which feature in the remainder of this book. Last, as will be evident, Olive Tree cannot be considered as a template for easy replication, given the scale and costs of what was involved. As an essentially unique version of cross-conflict dialogue, therefore, I deem it all the more important to record for general reference the findings Olive Tree delivered.

Ground Rules and Framing

In the first meeting of every new intake of scholars during my time as director, and at intervals thereafter, I explained that the participants were not expected to agree or asked to try to find agreement. The definition of success, I emphasised, was that all present would use the opportunity to gain a degree, with as high marks as possible, and learn as much as they could from the experience.

This last stipulation led naturally into discussion of the ground rules for the endeavour. Attendance at the weekly meetings during term time was mandatory, except in the case of illness or exceptional circumstances which had to be cleared with me. Everyone had to come to the 'retreats' and as it transpired no one wanted to miss the foreign trips anyway! However, sustained attendance over three years and throughout every session during the retreats was 'a big ask'. After all, even though leaving the region to spend time in London represented a sort of escape from the conflict, it was ever present in the dialogue sessions and everyone's identity was unavoidably bound up with it. No one could be detached.

Apart from mandatory attendance, another rule was that in all the full-group discussions the participants were expected to speak in English and not engage in side conversations. When working in sub-groups, on the occasions when these were not bi-national, they could converse in their native tongue, but were expected to revert to English when reporting back to the whole group or communicating with one or other of the facilitators.

In terms of giving each other time and space to articulate their views, reflections and questions, the participants were expected not to interrupt one another and to do their best to listen *and* hear. They were also enjoined to avoid using provocative statements or to 'disrupt or derail informative communication and the learning of others.' In the case of one cohort, following an outburst of acrimony, the participants formally agreed that thereafter each would: 'Try not to say what I need to say in a way I think could offend someone to the point they cannot stay in the room (because then there would be no point)'; and 'In so far as I can, *I* will stay in the room.' They also agreed to the statement: 'I did not come here to become someone I am not; someone *else*. I *did* come here to discuss the conflict in the region we are all from and to learn more about it.'

And: 'I undertake to reflect carefully before I speak and I agree to leave unsaid my personal judgements about other individuals in the group.'

It was also one of the ground rules that participants keep confidential what was said and by whom in any discussion and not relay to others outside the group (family, friends, whomever) what had been shared within the group. The importance of this stipulation became apparent to all the participants when they reflected on the implications for themselves of being quoted outside the meetings. In the course of an intense exchange of views, thoughts and feelings, people do say things spontaneously which help advance the discussion, but which could be considered highly personal or sensitive. So over time everyone becomes more invested in maintaining confidentiality for their own sake. Thus it is that a level of trust is built, but it takes a lot of time and can be lost all too quickly (see Chapter 5).

As will be apparent, the job of the facilitators was to 'hold' the group through the inevitable turbulence as well as the more enjoyable activities, exercises like simulations, outings to events and foreign trips. It is my understanding that all too often facilitators of cross-conflict dialogue can themselves fear discord and outbursts of anger. Yet it is incumbent upon them not to give into their fears, but rather to manage the dissonance and work with it in the interests of learning and discovery. The role of regular staff meetings and workshops was essential to keeping the facilitators on task and coordinated.

As I discovered, constrained by the ground rules from taking out their frustrations on each other, the dialogue participants may use the facilitators as a kind of punch bag. When they do not like the dissonance, they may accuse the facilitators of incompetence or insufficient appreciation of what they themselves have been forced to learn during the course of their lives in the conflict zone. The participants will also scrutinise the facilitators for any signs of tension between them, apparently acting on their fears that the whole endeavour could not 'hold' under duress. I also found participants tried repeatedly to tempt the facilitators to take sides or endorse one or other of the positions in contention.

I was helped by my colleagues, who have worked with students and other groups as psychotherapists, to understand this and other facets of group work, By way of example, I learned from them that every participant in a group exercise, not unlike members of a family, will find a role for themselves in the group – be it the one who seems to go out of their way to be combative, or who tries to avoid voicing their feelings at all, or purports not to care much – and the rest of the group come to rely on these roles being played out in the group.

Thus, if someone casts themselves in the role of the eternal sceptic who refuses to acknowledge any positive value in the exercise, that person may well become a scapegoat for what the other members of the group dislike about the exercise. The rest of the group can then think everything would be better if only this individual were not there. However, were that person actually to be excluded, then the group would simply try to find another scapegoat. Such are the facets of group work which serve the process of learning. And, by the way, those who did get cast as scapegoat in one or other cohort eventually gained a kind of acceptance, such that they ceased to be so invested in pursuing the spoiler role, and the whole group moved on to other concerns.

One of the lessons I learned from my work before Olive Tree, designing and running projects involving various nationalities, was that every project has a trajectory. Whether the lifespan of the project is one day, many months or several years, it is to be expected that at some point the proceedings will descend into confusion and uncertainty about what is being accomplished and where it is all going. The ideal is that the project participants start and end on a positive note, but are sustained through a difficult period in between. That difficult period actually means that complex issues are in fact being addressed and grappled with. Ultimate success therefore requires this muddled middle phase.

This was also my experience with each cohort of Olive Tree scholars and since the life span of that project was three years (for each cohort), the difficult phase tended to begin at the end of the first year or the beginning of the second. This was the stage at which the participants began to experience the dissonance that would portend the most substantial learning.

The Discoveries made through Group Work

For all the Olive Tree cohorts, the initial phase of their experience was about orientation. Typically, in their first term, the agenda featured many meetings with experts on different facets of the conflict along with attendance at events in London where panellists would pronounce their views. This usefully served to enable the Olive Tree scholars to find their own voices. They invariably found something to criticize or disagree with in all the expert views. Consequently, by the beginning of the second term they were ready for something different and to take more initiative themselves.

In the case of the third cohort, what happened next was not planned in advance, but did become the template for the subsequent two cohorts. Thus it was that the Olive Tree generated the main findings recounted in this book.

Responding to the mood in the group, my co-facilitators and I decided to initiate an exploration of the values the group members had been introduced to as children. Working in pairs or threesomes, the scholars were invited to compare notes on the fairy tales and nursery rhymes they had grown up with. Their task was to identify the defining characteristics of the heroines and heroes, the victims and victors, the authority figures and rebels, in the stories.[9] Both the Israelis and the Palestinians had been brought up with some of the classics, at least through Disney films, if not the books. Their views on these classics were quite similar. For example, both Palestinian and Israeli women were generally disdainful of the female characters, such as *Cinderella*, whose main goal in life appeared to revolve around marrying a prince.[10] That said, they saw the point of scrutinising the stories for their underlying messages and depictions of role models or characters to emulate.

Aside from the classics familiar in the West, the Israelis and Palestinians recollected different folk tales specific to their respective cultures and traditions. Interestingly, it emerged that in Palestinian homes it was often a grandmother who would be the storyteller for children, and they would embellish the stories with local references and details that a child could relate to. Rocky terrain, winding paths, woods, olive groves, wicked witches and magic spells, were among the features of such tales. Several of the Palestinians were apparently also given graphic depictions of hell to persuade them to be good children. Among the Israelis, by contrast, their memories were less of verbal storytelling and more of stories being read to them from illustrated books. Tales featuring the cultural heritage of their grandparents, be that in Europe, North Africa, Russia or wherever, appear not to have featured much. Nor was much said about relatives lost

---

[9] For insights on the value of fairy tales, see Bruno Bettelheim (1991) *The Uses of Enchantment: The Meaning and Importance of Fairy Tales*. Penguin. Bettelheim explains how fairy tales are more satisfying to children than fables and myths, in which the heroes are superhuman and to be emulated, but thereby cannot be identified with in the way that the characters in fairy tales can be. While fables carry explicit moralistic messages, fairy tales carry implicit messages about possibilities.

[10] Bettelheim has a more discerning take on gender roles in fairy tales, see *Ibid.*, pp.113-15. He also explains how attainment of royal status, something seemingly beyond the reach of ordinary mortals, is actually simply a metaphor for the attainment of success and is intended as a message of hope.

in the Holocaust, unless a child specifically asked about that.

In any case, the exercise of examining children's stories turned out to lead naturally into a discussion of the national narratives with which the students had each become familiar as they grew up, through the media and in school. As had been the case with the fairy tales they recollected, their memories featured visual images that had made an impression on them. Such images also tell a story of course and leave an imprint in the mind, which is their power.[11] The images most often chosen were of photographs depicting moments in the history of the conflict. Israeli and Palestinian interpretations of such images turned out to be starkly contrasting. For example, the famous picture of a small boy catapulting a stone at a seemingly advancing tank was understood as the little guy defiantly standing his ground in the face of a powerful enemy from which Palestinians, but not the Israelis, could take heart.

So it was that the Olive Tree participants began to identify their respective and contrasting understandings of the seminal moments and events in their shared past. The coexistence of alternative stories or versions of that past, operating in parallel, became manifest.

The next stage in the journey of discovery then unfolded. Working in pairs from one or other nationality, the scholars set about investigating their respective national narratives on different episodes in the course of the conflict. First, they compiled a list of the key episodes or turning points, including the events of 1948, 1967, 1973, the first Intifada and the second Intifada. Next, having agreed on one of these to focus on, they set about researching what they understood as the mainstream national narrative of their community on that episode. This meant reviewing what was written in the textbooks they had used at school and various internet sources, as well as interviewing family members and friends. Then, the students took it in turns to give illustrated presentations to the rest of the group.

The scholars were enjoined to make the presentation of their side's national narrative, or that of one or other sub-national community (such as religious Jewish settlers on the one hand or Gazan Palestinians on the other) as clear and compelling as possible, *but not to voice their own opinions.* They were to avoid using 'we' or 'our' and instead *report* on what the prevailing narrative was.

---

[11] See Galai, Y. (2019) 'The Victory Image: Imagining Israeli Warfighting from Lebanon to Gaza' *Security Dialogue*, 0967010619835365.

This proved to be the most potent phase in the learning exercise. The scholars uncovered things about their own side's narrative that they had not thought much about before. They did not necessarily agree or identify with everything they found. Plus, the experience gave them (and me) a new appreciation of how national narratives work. Crucially, when they also listened to and watched the presentations of the others in the group, they had a new appreciation of the coexistence of several internally coherent, deeply held and fundamentally incompatible narratives. This marked a breakthrough in their understanding of 'truth' and 'facts' – as discussed further in Chapter 4.

The group discussions and exercises did not end at this point, but this exercise set the scene for further explorations, including examining 'national values' and the ways in which the different communities perceived certain concepts or emotions like fear, courage, 'refugeeness', the military, victimhood, victory and so on.

Throughout, it was also the case that developments in the conflict 'back home' impinged on all the scholars and necessitated the development of strategies by myself and the other Olive Tree staff to help the scholars cope with anxiety, anger and pain. On this there will be more to say in Chapter 5.

The Survey Design

My main purpose in this chapter thus far has been to explain *the context* in which and *the process* by which not only the students but I too came to make our main discoveries. Above all else, we learned that the competing national narratives interpret 'the facts' differently. Such narratives are not fables or total inventions, but provide essentially subjective as opposed to universal understandings of 'the truth.' They define 'self' and 'other' and they shape the choices of the protagonists in the conflict accordingly.

Building on these discoveries, I decided to design a survey exercise to explore further and to gather more evidence on the distinctions between the Israeli and Palestinian narratives as internalised by comparable groups of young adults on both sides, rather than as propounded by their respective leaderships. I also wanted to see if I could identify any differences between the narratives as espoused by the participants in the Olive Tree and as embraced by comparable groups of Israelis and Palestinians who had not gone through the Olive Tree learning curve.

Specifically, I wanted to:

1. Identify common features in the conflict narratives of all the Palestinians surveyed
2. Identify common features in the conflict narratives of all the Israelis surveyed
3. Compare and contrast (1) and (2)
4. Compare and contrast Olive Tree Israeli conflict narratives with non-Olive Tree Israeli narratives
5. Compare and contrast Olive Tree Palestinian conflict narratives with non-Olive Tree Palestinian narratives
6. Compare and contrast successive 5th cohort conflict narratives across 4 sets of responses (from November 2014 to July 2016) – a longitudinal study – to monitor evolution of thinking during the Olive Tree experience.

Among the hypotheses I wanted to test were the following:

1. There will be common features across all the Israeli responses on the one hand and all Palestinian responses on the other hand – yielding 2 broad parallel national narratives.
2. That 'self' and 'other' are present in both parallel narratives – that is, both narratives are binary and the 'other' which features in each of the 2 national narratives will 'mirror' (as in reverse) the depictions of self.
3. The 'other' in the Israeli narrative will not be exclusively Palestinian – it could also be non-Jews for example.
4. The 'other' in the Palestinian narrative will be predominantly Jewish Israelis.
5. There will be discernible differences between Olive Tree responses and non-Olive Tree responses
6. There will be discernible differences between the first and the last sets of responses of the 5th cohort Olive Tree scholars.

As this last hypothesis indicates, the students enrolled in the fifth cohort of Olive Tree (from 2013-16) were asked to do the survey a total of four times, the first three times in English and at yearly intervals (in November 2013, 2014 and 2015) and one final time, in Arabic or Hebrew, in July 2016. It was at this last point, in July 2016 that all the other alumni of Olive Tree (48 in total) were also invited to take the survey – which yielded responses from 10 Jewish Israelis and

11 Palestinian alumni, the former in Hebrew and the latter in Arabic.

The groups of non-Olive Tree Jewish Israelis and Palestinians, selected for comparison with the Olive Tree respondents – what I have called the 'comparator' groups – were also surveyed in July 2016, in Hebrew and Arabic respectively. The former were all university graduates in their thirties, unknown to me, affiliated to an Israeli 'think tank' in Tel Aviv and recruited for the task by one of the senior fellows at the think tank. The Palestinian respondents were university students or graduates and unknown to me, aged in their twenties and thirties, affiliated to a Palestinian 'think tank' in the West Bank. They were recruited for this task by the senior staff of the think tank in the same manner as they periodically assembled 'focus groups' to test public opinion.

The data sets thus assembled were as follows:

a   Survey responses of 10 (Jewish) Israeli alumni of Olive Tree, completed July 2016.

b   Survey responses of 8 (Jewish) Israelis who did not experience Olive Tree, completed July 2016.

c   Survey responses of 11 Palestinian alumni of Olive Tree, completed July 2016.

d   Transcript of survey responses of 14 Palestinians who did not experience Olive Tree, completed in a 'focus group' format in July 2016.

e   3 sets of survey responses of 10 Olive Tree scholars from 5th cohort (4 Israelis and 6 Palestinians - 2 of whom Israeli citizens) completed at yearly intervals (Nov 2013, Nov 2014 and Nov 2015) and done in English.

f   Survey responses of 4 (Jewish) Israelis from 5th cohort completed in Hebrew, July 2016.

g   Survey responses of 6 Palestinians (2 of whom Israeli citizens) from 5th cohort completed in Arabic, July 2016.

The questionnaire administered in all cases was as reproduced in the box on the next page.

As will be evident, the circumstances in which each and every participant in this survey provided their responses were not exactly the same. However, the design of the exercise was sufficiently robust to yield a body of material that was more than sufficient to serve the intended purpose. Two of the Olive Tree alumni, one a Palestinian and the other an Israeli, and who did not themselves take the survey, were paid to translate the responses into English. The anonymity of the respondents was protected throughout.

Further, since there are no 'correct' answers to any of the questions, the responses encompass a set of personally held conflict narratives that, taken together, give a substantive insight into the perspectives and assumptions of well-educated young adults of roughly the same generation on opposite sides of the conflict. What they said in answer to my ten questions is used to inform and advance the discussion in each of the remaining chapters of this book. The findings overall are provided in the final chapter.

Questionnaire – translated into Arabic and Hebrew

Please write this 'off the top of your head' – don't stop to look things up or discuss with others. Please write between 1 (minimum) and 6 (maximum) pages…you have up to one hour to complete this

Tell the story (narrative) of the Israeli-Palestinian Conflict and "Peace Process" to date, as you see them, covering:

1. How far back – to what date/era do we need to go to identify the origins of the conflict?
2. What are the origins of the conflict?
3. Who are the Israelis?
4. Who are the Palestinians?
5. Are there any other actors/parties involved in the origins of the conflict?
6. If so, who are they and what was their role over time?
7. What do the Palestinians want now?
8. What do the Israelis want now?
9. Did the Oslo Peace Process fail? If yes, why? If not, what did it achieve?
10. What should happen now?

3
Self and Other

As we navigate through life, we each arrive at an understanding of our national or group identity. The process starts in childhood and continues through adulthood. What it means to be English as opposed to Scottish, Palestinian as opposed to Iraqi, Israeli as opposed to American, is something we discover incrementally through experience and enculturation. Our journey of discovery is informed by the social arrangements and institutions that frame every aspect of our lives, from our family, to the schools we attend, to the governing authorities whose laws determine our individual and group rights and responsibilities. Each of us learn how much power or agency we have, to choose our roles in society, and how much we are circumscribed by prevailing institutional factors, location, relative wealth, skin colour and so on.

For the participants in the Olive Tree Programme, their encounter with 'the other' during their time in London enabled them to reflect on aspects of their identity hitherto taken for granted. Their awareness of what it means to be Jewish and Israeli, Palestinian and Muslim or Christian, became more sharply focused. The relative benefits and constraints of belonging to one or other of these distinctive categories was frequently discussed between them.

According to Benedict Anderson,[1] the process by which Europeans have come to see themselves as belonging to different nationalities can be traced back to the invention of the printing press and thence the beginning of mass communication. That process has been driven in part by the opportunism of political elites, who saw the embrace of competing nationalisms as a way to mobilize communities and establish authority. In due course, the ideas of 'the nation-state', 'national sovereignty' and 'self-determination' and what constitutes 'legitimate' authority have entered common parlance and shaped global politics.

For the peoples of the Middle East, the notion of self-determination received a powerful endorsement, when US President Woodrow Wilson outlined his 'Fourteen Points' in January 1918. His purpose was to identify US objectives

---

[1] Anderson, B. ((2006) *Imagined Communities: Reflections on the Origin and Spread of Nationalism* London: Verso.

in the region which had hitherto come under the rule of the Ottoman Empire and to send a warning to the imperial powers of Europe who aspired to carve up the region between them. In Point Twelve Wilson said:

> The Turkish portions of the present Ottoman empire should be assured a secure sovereignty, but the other nationalities which are now under Turkish rule should be assured an undoubted security of life and an absolutely un-molested opportunity of autonomous development.[2]

The exact meaning of Wilson's remarks have been debated since then, and a strong case made that he did not envisage equality for the peoples of the Middle East on a par with that he espoused for the peoples of North America and Europe. However, be that as it may, Wilson's pronouncement did strike a different note to those of the European imperialists.

By 1918, Arab nationalist forces were already arrayed on the battlefield against the Turks, alongside the British, and Zionist aspirations had received the blessing of the British in the Balfour Declaration. Exactly where and how a distinctive Palestinian Arab national consciousness was also in evidence by this point has been in dispute between the Palestinians and the Israelis ever since.

Each of them have sought to trump the other in terms of the longevity, and thence purported legitimacy, of their claim to sovereignty over the land in dispute between them. Yet the manner in which they each define their national belonging or group identity stands in direct contradiction to the notions of either equality or compromise between them, as will become clear in the discussion which follows.

Self-identification is not to be confused with how either community is categorised by others. As Brubaker and Cooper warn, 'identity' is a slippery term and in the analyses of many scholars it has been used to mean everything and nothing much, in multiple and contradictory ways.[3] However, *as used in common parlance* the term is sufficient unto itself and beyond that, scholars are advised to use the terms 'identification', 'categorisation' and 'self-understanding' to distinguish between the labels we embrace and those foisted upon us. After all, as

---

[2] Fromkin, D. (2001) *A Peace to End All Peace: The Fall of the Ottoman Empire and the Creation of the Modern Middle East* New York: Owl Books, p.258.

[3] Brubaker, R. and Frederick Cooper (2000) "Beyond "Identity"", *Theory and Society* 29: 1-47.

Brubaker and Cooper point out, in any polity: 'the state monopolizes, or seeks to monopolize, not only legitimate physical force but also legitimate symbolic force'.[4]

How the state or absence of a state features in Israeli and Palestinian descriptions of themselves and the other is a central finding of this study, as revealed below. First though, there are a few more conceptual issues to clarify or emphasise, and this can be done by reference to the works of Palestinian and Israeli scholars who have investigated the subject of their respective national identities.

In the preface to his book *Palestinian Identity: the Construction of Modern National Consciousness*, Rashid Khalidi states: 'If one takes identity as the answer to the question: "Who are you?" it is clear that the response of the inhabitants of Palestine has changed considerably over time.'[5] With these words Khalidi establishes the centrality of self-identification in his account of the evolution of Palestinian national consciousness *and*, in so doing, he dismisses the notion that nationality is an intrinsic, fixed or essentialist identifier of a person or people. Quoting Anthony Smith, Khalidi explains: 'the nation that emerges in the modern era must be regarded as both a construct and process.'[6]

In his book, *The Invention and Decline of Israeliness*, Baruch Kimmerling[7] traces the evolution of Zionism as a Jewish national movement dedicated to founding a state for the Jews, with its own armed forces and labourers, led by a secular elite of European origins. Zionism was thus a quest for self-determination in the form of a state. Yet, as Kimmerling argues, the orientation and vision of the founders of that state in Palestine have, over time, been marginalised or displaced by the emergence of competing and overlapping Israeli self-identifications, including that of the religious nationalists, especially after the Israeli conquests of 1967. In the process, he demonstrates that Israeli national consciousness is neither monolithic nor immutable over time.

Citing poll data on the attitudes of Jewish and Arab-Israeli school-chil-

---

[4] Brubaker and Cooper (2000), p.15.

[5] Khalidi, R. (1997) *Palestinian Identity: The Construction of Modern National Consciousness* New York: Columbia University Press, p. viii.

[6] Khalidi (1997) p. xii.

[7] Kimmerling, B. (2005) *The Invention and Decline of Israeliness: State, Society, and the Military* Berkeley, Los Angeles & London: University of California Press.

dren, Yair Auron finds that: 'Since 1967, secular and religious Zionist circles alike have experienced an intensification of radical nationalist trends. This has often taken the form of xenophobic nationalism, rejection of the (non-Jewish) other and an unwillingness to recognize the rights of the other party to the conflict.'[8]

This notion of 'self and other' is explained by Edward Said in the Afterword to the 1995 edition of his book *Orientalism*:

> The construction of identity – for identity, whether of Orient or Occident, France or Britain, while obviously a repository of distinct collective experiences, *is* finally a construction – involves establishing opposites and 'others' whose actuality is always subject to the continuous interpretations and reinterpretations of their differences from 'us'. Each age and society re-creates its 'Others'. Far from a static thing, then, identity of 'self' or of 'other' is a much worked-over historical, social, intellectual, and political process that takes place as a contest involving individuals and institutions in all societies.[9]

As Auron sees it: 'the decades that have passed since the establishment of Israel have witnessed the evolution of an "oppositional identity" that developed in opposition to the terrible Holocaust; in opposition to the Arabs, who attempt to undermine our very existence; and in opposition to the world, which is allegedly entirely against us.'[10]

In their works, both Khalidi and Kimmerling also discuss how the notion of 'self' is informed by contact with 'the other' *and* the conflict. That said, Khalidi is at pains to point out that the Zionists, and subsequently the Israelis, were not the only 'other' depicted in Palestinian discourse. The Arabs in other parts of the region, in the Arab states created by the British and French after World War I, were a reference point for the Palestinians, not least because they, unlike the Palestinians, were allowed representative bodies by the colonialists in their respective states and eventually won independence. Palestinian intellectu-

---

[8] Auron, Y. (2012) *Israeli Identities: Jews and Arabs Facing Self and the Other* New York and Oxford: Berghahm Books, p.18.

[9] Said, E. (2003) *Orientalism* London: Penguin, p.332.

[10] Auron (2012), p.153.

als were inspired by broader Arab nationalism, but later felt betrayed, following the Arab defeats of 1967, and the various accommodations with Israel (and the Americans) made by the Arab states thereafter.[11]

Kimmerling, meanwhile, discusses how Zionism originally emerged as a response to the rise of different European national identities in the nineteenth and twentieth centuries and how the Israelis continue to seek recognition and acceptance as a Western-style democracy, thereby distinguishing themselves from all the dictatorial Arab states in their neighbourhood. Kimmerling also accords central importance to the continuation of the Israeli-Palestinian conflict in Israeli political culture, such that: 'war-making has not only become the state's ethos and the central binding code of a fragmented, pluralistic, cultural system, but even incorporates peace-making as part and parcel of itself.'[12]

For Khalidi, the successive defeats suffered by the Palestinians over the years have not produced a culture of 'victimhood' (though others regard this as a given[13]), so much as an ethos of 'steadfastness' in the face of insuperable odds. He asserts that, for the Palestinians maintenance of their distinctive national identity has become their affirmation in the absence of a state.[14]

Thus it is that various scholars have provided pointers for what to look for in the self-understandings of Israelis and Palestinians and thereby set the scene for the main focus of this chapter. That is, to look at how the Israelis and Palestinians who participated in the survey exercise I undertook, defined themselves and the other.

The details of that survey are provided in Chapter 2 and I shall not repeat those details here, but I do want to emphasise that the respondents could in no way be considered representative samples of their respective societies. The respondents were, however, comparable with one another in so far as they were drawn from among those Israelis and Palestinians who were awarded Olive Tree scholarships and who were exposed to contact with each other in a di-

[11] For more on this see Anziska, S. (2018) *Preventing Palestine: A Political History from Camp David to Oslo* Princeton and Oxford: Princeton University Press.

[12] Kimmerling pp.14-15 and see also pp.87 and 124.

[13] See Smulders, K.N. (2013) 'The Battle over Victimhood: Roles and Implications of Narratives of Suffering in the Israeli-Palestinian Conflict' in Matar, D. and Zahera Harb, eds., *Narrating Conflict in the Middle East* London: I.B. Tauris, pp.164-182.

[14] Khalidi, pp.198-201.

alogue exercise that ran parallel to their degree programmes over a period of three years. Their responses to my questions are also compared here with those of two 'comparator groups',[15] one Israeli and one Palestinian, made up of graduates, in their twenties and thirties, the former living and working in Tel Aviv and the latter in or near various cities in the West Bank.

In what follows I focus on the respondents' answers to two questions: 'Who are the Israelis?' and 'Who are the Palestinians?' The factors or themes which feature in their responses include the attributes of statehood, such as citizenship and service in the armed forces, and of statelessness, such as refugeeness and resistance. They also make reference to history, geography, language and religion among other facets of self-identification. Also examined is the extent to which the respondents' descriptions of their own national group reference the other and the conflict. Some of their descriptions of the other constitute a mirror image or opposite of how they see themselves. Up to a point, their depictions of self and other are therefore binary or co-dependent.

Israeli Self-Identification:
The recurring themes of Judaism and statehood

Here are some examples of how Israeli respondents answered the question 'Who are the Israelis?' The first three came from the 'comparator group', and next three from Olive Tree alumni.

Three non-Olive Tree Israeli Responses

1. Most of the Israelis are Hebrew speaking Jews, whose origins can be traced back to different countries around the world and who have a religious or historical affinity with Judaism. Today, these Jews live in the state of Israel as citizens. They hold a blue Teudat Zehut [*ID*] and have the right to vote. Most of them pay taxes and serve (or have served) in the military. There is also a group of a few hundred thousand 'Israelis' who live in different countries around the world. These are Israeli citizens who left Israel (or their parents left Israel), temporarily or permanently, for different reasons and who continue to have a strong affinity to Israel. Some of them even form their own communities, distinct from the 'Jewish communities' in the countries where they live.

---

[15] For details of which see Chapter 2, pp. 48-51≠.

2. The Israeli identity developed from the Jewish identity. The Jews lived all around the world for thousands of years and maintained a joint ethnic and religious identity. And as the European national awakening took place, the Jews who lived in European countries became influenced by the rise of national ideas. These national ideas gave birth to the Zionist idea (that is, the idea of a Jewish nationality) which turned the Jews from an ethnic-religious group into a nation. Like all other national movements, the Zionist movement worked towards the establishment of a state unit for its nation. At its core, the goal of Zionism was the return of the Jews to, and the establishment of a national home in, Eretz Israel. The Zionist idea led to waves of Aliya and to Jews settling in Eretz Israel. Simultaneously, the Zionist leadership worked towards gaining international and political recognition for the establishment of a Jewish national home – a state, or some sort of a state unit – for the Jewish people. Following the end of the Second World War, and because of the Holocaust, a new political situation was created – an international recognition of the need for establishing a Jewish state emerged. This was needed in order to provide the survivors of the Holocaust with a place of refuge, but also in order to fix an historical injustice in which a national group [*i.e. the Jews*] was denied a geographical area in which it could live in independence. Following the establishment of the state of Israel, the Israeli identity was created and the residents of the state began calling themselves 'Israelis'.

3. Jews who are returning to their homeland, from which they were exiled 2,000 years ago.

Three Israeli Olive Tree Alumni Responses

1. An Israeli is anyone who holds a blue Israeli ID card [*Teudat Zehut*]. This includes the Jews and Arabs who lived inside the borders of Israel before it was established and who remained there, as well as the Jews who made Aliya to Israel after it was established and their descendants.

2. From a civilian perspective, a mixed society comprised of a majority and minorities, of preferences and discrimination. It is a very united society on the one hand but a very disturbed one on the other. And when I say united, this is as long as the person at hand is on the 'right' side

of the political map. As in, if they are part of the majority. It is a very frightened society, always has been. It always functions under a fear for its own existence. However, over the past few years, in responding to outside attacks, the Israeli society has become more radical and aggressive and less tolerant, and it is heading towards losing its character as a democratic society. When it comes to the conflict specifically, the Israeli society is not the mixed society it alleges to be. The minorities, for example the Palestinian minority (which encompasses 20% of the population), is not a part of that society. In this context, the Israelis are Jewish citizens of Israel.

3. The Israelis, by definition, are those living inside the territory of the state of Israel, under Jewish sovereignty. Today, the Israeli society is multifaceted and it is internally divided and torn-up. There is no doubt that two generations on, following the generation of the founders, being Israeli no longer signifies only one thing. Nevertheless, the Israelis are interested in living in peace over the land of the state of Israel, the only question remaining is how big this land is.

My reading of all twenty-two[16] Israeli responses to the question 'Who are the Israelis?' is that they actually form a relatively coherent mix, encompassing the following range of definitions: those who hold Israeli citizenship and/or live in the state of Israel and 'feel Israeli'; citizens in Israel since 1948; mostly Hebrew-speaking Jews with Israeli ID, who pay taxes and serve in the IDF, including those not currently living in Israel; those who made Aliya; and Jews and Zionists and 'allies who are willing to carry the burden of the good of the state of Israel (including Druze and a minority of the Christian Arabs)'.

There was one variation on this mix, namely: 'Jews who are returning to their homeland from which they were exiled 2,000 years ago'. That was the only response which could be considered to reflect the discourse of religious nationalists, but as noted previously, the sample was not representative of all sectors of Israeli society and those surveyed included no ultra-Orthodox and only a few observant Jews. That said, as discussed by Kimmerling in his work, secular and even atheist Jews refer to the Bible to underpin the national connection to the

---

[16] See categories of respondents, Chapter 2 pp. 48-51.

land of Israel.

As illustrated in the examples above, some respondents pointed out that the citizens of Israel include non-Jews, though Jewishness featured as the main defining characteristic of 'the Israelis' in all the responses. In so far as they saw fit to try to define the Jews, the respondents mentioned nationality, ethnicity, the survivors of the Holocaust and/or religion. Zionism was also mentioned by several.

The other main defining feature of the Israeli responses was citizenship of the state of Israel. Particularly noteworthy was the sense of commitment which many respondents equated with belonging to the Israeli identity and for them this appeared to mean national or military service. No one referred to the Palestinian 'other' directly, though the conflict featured obliquely, including in terms of a sense of being under threat.

Comparing the Olive Tree alumni responses with those of the comparator group, the former mixed together state- and citizenship-related depictions with an emphasis on the psychological dimensions of 'Israeliness'. Their responses included the following range of definitions: affinity to Judaism; holding Israeli citizenship/ID; those who understand themselves as Israeli (and are misunderstood by everyone else); collective consciousness of a people persecuted/victimized, beleaguered and/or expelled from homes elsewhere; and diaspora Jews for whom Israel is a 'second home'. To me these Olive Tree responses do not speak of self-confidence but rather of somewhat troubled reflection.

Israeli Depictions of the Palestinians

Turning to how the Israeli respondents answered the question 'Who are the Palestinians?' here are the responses of the same six Israelis quoted above.

Three non-Olive Tree Israeli Responses

1. The Palestinians are mostly Muslims (some of them are Christian) who speak Arabic and whose origins (two or three generations back) can be traced back to the geographical area of Eretz Israel (or Palestine). Some of them live in different countries around the world (mostly in different Arab countries; many of them live in Jordan, but some also live in European or Northern American countries) while others live in Israel's area, under Israeli rule (inside the Green line) or outside of it, or in the territories which are under Palestinian control (West Bank and

Gaza). The Palestinians have a historical and a geographical affinity to the territory of the state.

2. The Palestinians are the Arab residents who lived in the area of Palestine and who began developing a national identity following the beginning of the Jewish settlement. At the beginning, this identity was not fully consolidated, and it sided with the other Arab nations in the area. Following the establishment of the state of Israel, and after the Arab states proved unsuccessful in their attempt to foil the Zionist idea, the Palestinians began developing their own independent identity. The formation of this identity also constituted a part of their war against the state of Israel. Starting from the 1950s, and even more so following the defeat of the Arab States during the Six Day war in 1967, the Palestinians felt that they weren't only being 'led' by the Arab states in their struggle, but that they are leading it themselves. Thus, the development of an Arab national identity accelerated, and a particular local identity was formed – the Palestinian identity.

3. The inhabitants of the area [*literally, the sons of the area – translator's note*] who are not Jews and who lived in the land called 'Palestine'.

Three Israeli Olive Tree Alumni Responses

1. The Palestinians are the Arabs who lived inside the territory of Eretz Israel before 1948 and their descendants. This also includes all those who still live there today as well as those who ran away, or were expelled, outside of the territory of Eretz Israel. Since there is no Palestinian state yet.

2. A national, ethno-Arab group whose members live and/or lived in Mandatory Palestine (under the British Mandate rule), which is today Israel, the West Bank and Gaza (including the 1948 refugees). It is a group that came together under a joint identity umbrella out of tribes and smaller social orders, and this identity is based on belonging to a specific geographical area. National sentiment began forming in the period when empires began dissolving and nationalism became more prominent, but mostly as a response to the entrance of Zionist Jewish

nationalism to the area and to its perception as a threat. This too is a mixed society and, like the Israeli society, discrimination and exclusion, and pressures to join the majority which is moving towards radicalisation, exist in this society as well. When we talk about identities in the context of the conflict, this identity does not unambiguously refer to everyone, for example to Christian Palestinians in relation to negotiations regarding the holy sites. So, when it comes to negotiating the conflict, the Palestinians are Muslim Palestinians who live in the West Bank and Gaza.

3. The Palestinians are Arabs living in the territory of the state of Israel, in the Gaza Strip and in the West Bank. In addition, there are Palestinian refugees in Jordan. The Palestinians live under Israeli occupation and they are the ones suffering most from the conflict.

Of all the Israeli respondents there was one (not quoted here) who answered this and the previous question with a history of the conflict – implying a sense that the two peoples cannot be identified independently. The rest came up with definitions of the Palestinians that included: those who are residents of Judea and Samaria of Arab descent and Arab-Israelis; those who self-identify as Palestinian including those who are 'citizens' of Arab countries and 'regard' themselves as 'refugees' and those living elsewhere with some connection 'to this land'; those whose national identity was formed after/in relation to Jews in the 2nd Aliya[17]; those whose origins can be traced back to the pre-Israel land of Eretz Israel 'including those in territories which are under Palestinian control'; those Arabs who developed Palestinian Identity after 1948; and those non-Jews who lived 'in the land called "Palestine"'. Some respondents used the term 'expelled' to explain what happened to the Palestinians historically.

What stands out above all, however, is the difference between the responses from the comparator or non-Olive Tree group and those of the Olive Tree alumni. The former described the Palestinians in a manner which undermined or questioned the substance or authenticity of the Palestinian national identity, in marked contrast to the tones and terms in which they described their own

---

[17] From 1904 to 1910, see Black, I. (2017) *Enemies and Neighbours: Arabs and Jews in Palestine and Israel, 1917-2017* London: Allen Lane, p.33.

national identity. They depicted Palestinian national consciousness as a response to Jewish settlement and/or the establishment of the state of Israel and the failure of the Arab states to 'foil the Zionist idea' and as emerging decades after the formation of the Zionist movement.

The Olive Tree alumni, meanwhile, were both matter-of-fact in their descriptions of the Palestinians (referring to their Arabness, their location and their origins) and revealing of some appreciation of what Palestinians say about themselves. Though one alumnus did refer to them as those whose identity emerged after 1948; and another said the Palestinians formed their identity in reaction to events, especially Zionism – and also made a distinction between Christian and Muslim Palestinians.

Other alumni descriptions included: those resisting occupation and Israeli rule; descendants of refugees; those who self-identify as Palestinian; 'indigenous inhabitants (past and present) of the territories controlled by Israel and their descendants'; 'victims of the colonial aspects of the Zionist movement'; 'Arabs who were in the country from time immemorial, were born in the country and aspire to national independence and self-determination'; 'the local indigenous population of Palestine and those expelled in '48 and '67 and their descendants'; and those 'suffering most from the conflict'.

In sum, the alumni descriptions of the Palestinians suggest a stronger sense of a people with a grievance, a history and a cause that has credence. As such, they attributed substance and thence some authenticity to the Palestinian national identity notwithstanding the latter's failures to realise their national aspirations. Thus, while the comparator group responses depicted the Palestinians as losers and enemies, the alumni saw them as another or parallel movement to their own, with a cause as yet unattained.

Palestinian Self-Identification: Local origins, displacement and struggle

Below are some examples of how Palestinian respondents answered the question 'Who are the Palestinians?' The first three came from the 'comparator group' who were participants in a 'focus group'[18] and delivered their responses verbally and in a conversational or debating manner. The subsequent three were individual responses provided in writing by Olive Tree alumni.

---

[18] For more detail on this see Chapter 2, pp. 48-51.

Three non-Olive Tree Palestinian Responses

1. Palestinians are originally the Canaanites. We are the children of the Canaanites. We are the owners of the land. We came from the Philistine tribes and this is why we are called Palestinians. This shows the strong bond between the land and us and shows that we are the true owners of the land. This is our origin.

2. The question should be who called us Palestine? Who are the Palestinians? If each one of us would do a DNA test we would find genes from Yemen, the Caucasus, and the Arab Maghreb. This is the same everywhere around the world not just in Palestine. So, we should ask who called us Palestine? Are Palestinians only in the West Bank? They imposed on us a separate state in Gaza. When I go on Facebook I see comments from Westerners and even Arabs living in the West talking about Gaza as if Gaza isn't part of Palestine.

3. The Canaanites. We are not limiting the definition of the Canaanites to the Palestinians inside Palestine only. Some of them are in Jordan, Egypt and even outside the Arab world. This also means that Palestinians are not only those living in Palestine. Canaanites is a very general term we need to think about when answering. This is similar to the way we say Palestinians are Arabs.

Three Palestinian Olive Tree Alumni Responses

1. Palestinians are those who have Palestinian origin. Most of them are Arabs. A percentage of them live in the occupied land and Israel and a greater percentage of them are refugees in the Arab countries as well as migrants (those who decided to migrate and were not forced to). Originally they were a mixture of all the peoples and cultures that lived in the area called historic Palestine.

2. The Palestinians are the original inhabitants of Palestine that lived there before 1948 and their descendants. They are a group of people that are paying the price for other people's mistakes and sins. They are a group of people that are denied their rights despite the justness of their cause.

3. Palestinians are the people who were forced to leave their own houses during and after the *Nakba*. They are the people who are living in the diaspora, who cannot even return to visit their original houses. They are the people who are living in different parts of the country, whether it is the West Bank, Gaza or Israel. They are the people who are still struggling in their basic life. They do not have their basic life, they cannot move freely, they also do not have freedom of speech; as they cannot express their political opinion. Moreover, a very high percentage of Palestinians are either in Israeli jails, have demolished houses or have a family member who was shot or arrested at least once.

There were seventeen Palestinian alumni in total who gave individual responses and a further fourteen in the comparator 'focus' group. Their responses to the question 'Who are the Palestinians?' ranged from an historical account of Palestinian ancestry, to the people called Palestinians by others, to those who own the land and have prior rights to it. According to some members of the comparator group, Palestinians were originally Canaanites. As mentioned by one, in the distant past the Jews refused to fight the Canaanites. According to another, quoted above: 'We are the owners of the land. We came from the Philistine tribes and this is why we are called Palestinians. This shows the strong bond between the land and us and shows that we are the true owners of the land. This is our origin.'

Similar answers included: 'We own this land. We have been here for thousands of years and we shall remain here.' But according to another, the question is: 'Who called us Palestine?' and: 'The British called us Palestine. Before them it was the Levant.' One pondered what to make of the distinctions now drawn between Gaza, Jerusalem, and those originating from Hebron but living in Jordan, and said 'I'm talking about only 120 years ago…before then the Levant was connected'. There was also the simple assertion: Palestinians are 'the people living in the borders drawn by Britain.'

Another respondent reflected that Bedouins do not 'own' land, and said: 'Our ancestors came to this land, worked it and we became Palestnians. The land became ours when it was no one's.' Broadly, the respondents focused on defining the Palestinians in terms of their lineage and rights, especially to the land, and in so doing inferred that by predating the Zionists on the land of Palestine

65

their right to that land trumped that of the Israelis. As one Palestinian Olive Tree alumnus asserted: 'They are the people who lived in Palestine throughout its history.'

The response that most encapsulated the notion of rights coupled with commitment ran as follows: 'Palestinians are the only people who have the right to live in Palestine. There are a lot of consequences for calling oneself Palestinian. It means you have to be part of the people, part of the resistance, and one of the people who defend Palestine. This way you can [call] yourself Palestinian, become someone who has the right to the land and [call] Palestine your country.'

Of note among the alumni responses were a few who, like one of those quoted above, described the Palestinians in terms of their fate, as 'the losers'. Thus, according to another Olive Tree alumnus:

The Palestinians who lived in the imperial era were Arab Muslims. With the failure of the national project and national and socialist struggles against Israel the masses turned to Islamism and liberalism with each having their foreign loyalties. The Palestinians [are] too weak to have sovereignty and that's why their identity is part of a wider external struggle over power and Palestine. Imperialism is the main player in this.

Yet another Palestinian Olive Tree alumnus drew a distinction between two groups of Palestinians: One that has hope and believe that they will have justice and a country; and those that are working towards individual goals – a group that still fights and a group that 'adopted the occupation'. He/she added: 'the world needs to understand that there are different types of occupation in Jerusalem, the West Bank and Gaza.'

Overall, what stands out is that the comparator or non-Olive Tree group respondents were keenest to establish roots that go as far back as that of the Jews in the region. One may surmise that in this they were directly responding to claims frequently repeated in official Israeli discourse. By contrast, the Olive Tree alumni manifested a stronger sense of what they experienced (in comparison to their Israeli peers in the Olive Tree) as the unfairness of their fate and were more prone to describe themselves in terms of their collective suffering than their rights.

Palestinian Depictions of the Israelis

Moving on, here are some examples of how Palestinian respondents answered the question 'Who are the Israelis?' The first three came from the comparator group, and the subsequent three from Olive Tree alumni.

Three non-Olive Tree Palestinian Responses

1. They are, like someone else said, a product of the charade[19] of the Holocaust. They [*not specified, presumably non-Jewish Europeans – translator's note*] started displacing the Jews who suffered the Holocaust and other people who were scattered as citizens all over and brought them to Palestine. Not all the Israelis are originally Israelites.

2. We need to distinguish between the Israelites that were mentioned in the Holy Quran and the Israelis that exist today. The Israelites followed Moses in Egypt and the Quran described them as believers. They were faced with problems and we all know the story of Moses. Let's distinguish the Jews that live today from those who lived during the time of Moses. Those who lived in foreign countries, they were converted to Judaism like people were converted to Islam when it reached Europe and America. The Jews we are talking about at the moment, I call them Zionists. If you are a Zionist you can be called Israeli. The Israelites is a name the Zionists assumed, to give themselves a historic characteristic, nothing more. They are Zionists. We can replace Israelis with Zionists. This is better. I'm against calling it the Israeli entity and I want it to be called the Zionist entity. The Israelites are mentioned in the Quran. We know the Israelites and we read their story so why would we call these people Israelis? They are Zionists who gathered...[*the speaker was interrupted*]

3. They are a mixture of many European nationalities. They formed the nucleus for a state in Palestine. After that generation there was a new

---

[19] Palestinian use of the word 'charade' when referring to the Holocaust is not necessarily, according to the translator, a denial that the Holocaust took place, but is more likely a refusal to accept that the Holocaust proves that the Jews are a uniquely victimised and endangered people – which is a denial of the meaning attributed to the Holocaust by many.'

generation that believes in new things. They believe they have a right in Palestine. This is when the Palestinian-Israeli conflict started. They are not connected to the Israelites who existed during the time of Moses. They are totally different.

Three Palestinian Olive Tree Alumni Responses

1. The Israelis currently are those carrying an Israeli passport. Mostly they are Jews of European and African origins. The Israelis are now in Israel and before that they lived as citizens in their mother countries. There is a small percentage of Jews who lived continuously in Palestine.

2. A group of Zionists who believe in a racist ideology that advocates Jews are superior to all other races on earth. They are a group of colonialists who want to control a land that is not theirs by force and expel, kill and displace the Palestinians.

3. Israelis are the people who moved to Palestine after the *Nakba*. They are the people who believe in the existence of Israel and ignoring the fact that there were the Palestinian natives who have the right before then to live in Palestine. They are also the people who ignored the Palestinians' basic human rights and still serve in the army and violate people's rights and also give themselves the right to end others' life.

Taking all the non-Olive Tree Palestinian responses as a whole, three variations on a theme were in evidence. One was simply to assert that Judaism is not a nationality it is a religion. A second depicted the Israelis as the 'product of the charade of the Holocaust' and other people who were scattered and brought to Palestine. As stated by one respondent: 'Not all Israelis are originally Israelites'. Yet, according to this view they were minorities (at one stage it was asserted they were converts to Judaism) in many countries and what happened was that 'The world decided to get rid of them through establishing a state'.

The third variation had it that: There are two types of Israelis – 'the capitalists who believe this is their country' and the Jews. And: 'The Israelites is a name the Zionists assumed to give themselves a historic characteristic, nothing more. They are Zionists.' And finally: 'Lets distinguish the Jews that live today from those who lived during the time of Moses – whom the Quran described as "believers". Jews in foreign countries are converts.'

These responses portray a classic example of 'othering' indicative of lack of contact with or knowledge of Israelis as people, on an individual basis. They also manifest a desire to delegitimize Zionism and its claims and deny that contemporary Jewish Israelis originate from the 'the Israelites' mentioned in the Quran. The term 'charade of the Holocaust' is, according to the translator, one commonly used by Palestinians to dismiss Israeli claims, to statehood and the land, which invoke the Holocaust. The phrase was not used by any of the Olive Tree alumni, however, who had gained awareness of the offence it causes and may even have calculated that using it would diminish their own case.

One alumnus made a distinction between Jews and Zionists and settlers and the government – all people 'like us', who suffered the Holocaust, but then asked: 'why do they do to us what was done to them?' Another Olive Tree alumnus said: 'I'm supposed to consider the Israelis as two opposing things: On the one side they are "the other" whose existence prolongs the occupation and on the other side some of them are my friends who love and respect me.'

A less reflective response was: 'Israelis today are the people who are occupying the occupied territories in Palestine and hold Israeli citizenship.' Another simply stated the Israelis are 'the people who immigrated to Palestine in waves in the beginning of the 20th century'. Meanwhile, as illustrated in the responses of two of the Olive Tree alumni quoted above, exposure to facilitated discussion with 'the other' is no guarantee that such dialogue is an antidote to hostility.

Overall, it appears that only some of the alumni see the Israelis as people first and the enemy second. More tellingly, and in contrast to the comparator group respondents, some alumni described the Israelis as the ones who deprived 'us' of our land and rights and forced 'us' out – a very binary definition of self and other.

How Views *May* Evolve through Dialogue

In this section, I reflect on the evolution of the views of Israelis and Palestinians in the 5th Cohort, between November 2013 (2 months into their first undergraduate year at City and the Olive Tree experience) and July 2016 (when they had just graduated). In this cohort there were four Jewish Israelis, two Palestinians with Israeli passports, a Palestinian with East Jerusalem ID, two Gazan Palestinians and one from the West Bank.

In 2013 the Jewish Israeli respondents broadly sought to define 'the Israelis' in an inclusive way, as encompassing all those of whatever religion who live in Israel, hold Israeli ID and accept the laws of the state even if they do not identify with the national ideal. For instance, one said the Israelis are:

Citizens who relate in any way to the idea of a Jewish and democratic state in the land of Israel. They don't necessarily have to be Jewish, or even supportive of the notion of a Jewish state, but they must at least reconcile with Israel's Jewish character and abide by its democratic constitution.

By the finish, in 2016, however, these respondents defined 'the Israelis' more narrowly and in terms of those who *self-identify* as Israeli and mostly live in Israel – and who are divided among themselves on the parameters and geographic limits of their state. What this indicates is that the Israeli participants in the Olive Tree had 'heard' their Palestinian colleagues, especially those with Israeli passports, and understood that they do not self-identify as Israeli or even Arab-Israeli, but rather as Palestinians who happen to have Israeli passports.

The evolution demonstrated here is, I suggest, from a desire to demonstrate magnanimity and inclusiveness to a realisation – and acceptance – that it is not within their power to decide for other people.

In 2013, meanwhile, the Jewish Israeli respondents came up with a range of definitions of the Palestinians, related to Israeli statehood on the one hand and the absence of Palestinian statehood on the other. One respondent defined the Palestinians in the same words as he/she had previously defined the Israelis, simply substituting the word 'Palestinians' for 'Israelis', ending on an ambivalent note about who can be considered a Palestinian 'any more'. In effect, they could have been saying 'what's in a name?' and it all depends where you live; or, they could have been conveying confusion and displeasure at having to respond to this question. Another answered that the Palestinians are:

People who deserve to have their own country. They are resisting and fighting in order to build a state just like the Israelis did when they tried to do that. The Israelis built their nation on a land that was partly Palestinian before and was occupied by Israel in the independence war after the Palestinians rejected the UN partition plan for Palestine.

By the finish, in 2016, the Israeli responses reflected how the Palestinians themselves self-identify. In this sense the respondents forbore to try to define 'the other' and simply reported what they had learned. One response ran as follows:

> Those who define themselves as Palestinians. They do not necessarily have a Palestinian ID and are not necessarily born in the territories considered today as belonging to the Palestinian Authority. There are Palestinians who also meet the definition of 'Israelis', and yet, as I've discovered over the past few years, they consider themselves Palestinians. Who am I to interfere with that?

In their 2013 responses the Palestinians in this cohort conveyed some discomfort with the question and an awareness that 'Israeliness' is more a construction than an essence. Thus, one respondent said Israelis are an invented concept, their 'unity' is an invention, and that 'unity of blood' is racist. Another answered in a way reflective of both duality and ambiguity:

> Israelis? Are who took 'my' land, Israelis are the ones who gave me an Israeli passport and ID but still treat me as a refugee rather than a citizen. Israelis are my friends I met, and became part of my life. Israelis are my enemy.

This awareness of the duality and ambiguity was still apparent in the responses of 2016. One Palestinian said the Israelis are 'just people like me brought up to whitewash what happened to Palestinians' and not fundamentally different beings, and wondered why, therefore, they repeat the sins committed against them against others. A third said:

> I'm supposed to consider the Israelis as two opposing things. On the one side they are the other whose existence prolongs the occupation and on the other side some of them are my friends who love and respect me.

Yet others described the Israelis as 'the other' in simple binary terms like:

> The Israelis are the people that were created after the 1948 *Nakba*. It's limited to Jews. The Israelis today are the people who are occupying the occupied territories in Palestine and hold the Israeli citizenship. They also

adhere to Zionist ideology.

Overall there is a contrast between those respondents prepared to let their personal experience of their Israeli colleagues inform their answers and those who do not want 'to go there' and stick to the impersonal. It is notable though that the respondent who referred to some Israelis as friends 'who love and respect me' did not choose to say whether these sentiments were reciprocated. I am reminded here of one Olive Tree discussion in which Damian invited the participants to consider the questions: Can your enemy also be your friend? Can you 'friend' your way out of conflict? And: Are there red lines or limits? The ensuing discussion revealed a strong sense that befriending someone from the other side in the conflict is problematic and fraught with reservations.

Turning to how the Palestinians of the fifth cohort defined themselves, in 2013 their responses were about what the Palestinians *feel* and their sense of victimhood. The Palestinians are alone and suffering. They have been duped and taken advantage of by Jewish migrants; they are victims of Western perfidy and 'many' massacres, and they are the prior inhabitants of the land. Thus, I discern, the Palestinians *arrived* in London with a strong sense of the unfairness of their lot and the deprivations that they suffer and, as it turned out, this sense was not ameliorated by dialogue.

On the contrary, by the end, in 2016, this sense of the unfairness and the contrast between what they lack and what others, not least their Israeli counterparts have, had, if anything become even more pronounced. Several said it should be no surprise the Palestinians resort to violence. The most comprehensive response, quoted earlier, bears repeating. It ran:

> Palestinians are the people who were forced to leave their own houses during and after the *Nakba*. They are the people who are living in the diaspora, who cannot even return to visit their original houses. They are the people who are living in different parts of the country, whether it is the West Bank, Gaza or Israel. They are the people who are still struggling in their basic life. They do not have their basic life, they cannot move freely, they also do not have freedom of speech, as they cannot express their political opinion. Moreover a very high percentage of Palestinians are either in jails, have demolished houses or have a family member who was shot or arrested at least once.

Overall, these Palestinians started out with strong feelings about the sequence of tragedies that befell the Palestinians and the injustice and unfairness of it all. They ended more in anger than in sadness – reeling off a litany of the constraints and the absences of basic freedoms that define the lot of the Palestinians today.

To conclude, in brief, the main themes to emerge from the survey with respect to self-identification, irrespective of exposure to dialogue, were: the achievement of statehood versus the failure to attain it; competing definitions of entitlement based on relative levels and types of suffering and the longevity of a presence in the land; and disagreement over the derivations and thence authenticity of national or group consciousness. Focusing specifically on the responses of the Olive Tree alumni, meanwhile, what stands out is that, through dialogue, the Israelis appear to have gained a greater appreciation of the Palestinian perspective, while the Palestinians were reinforced in their sense of relative deprivation. Thus, dialogue may shift some perceptions and intensify others.

4

National Narratives

Our national narratives are the stories we are told and we tell our children which give meaning to our national identities. They draw on collective memories, historical experiences, seminal texts and folk tales from which we derive meanings and values. They explain what distinguishes 'us' from 'others' and they feature our heroic deeds, our friends and enemies, our aspirations and our fears.

All national narratives evolve over time. They adapt to incorporate new events and experiences – wars, plagues, invasions, tsunamis and revolutions. They also change 'to fit the current needs of the group'[1] and to reflect the agendas of those in power at the time. National governments make it their business to try to shape the story that distinguishes their people and their state from others. They construct monuments, designate national holidays, identify national icons, adopt a national anthem and determine which cultural artefacts are most celebrated. They also pay attention to what children learn at school.[2] These are all facets of state-building, important for the legitimacy of the state and the support of the people.[3]

This does not mean that political authorities have complete control over the national narrative of a state or people. Everyone who identifies with the nation plays a part in shaping its story and collective memory. The authorities may write the official script, but the people – the actors in the drama – may forget their lines, make up new ones, improvise, and conjure up new meanings. In any case the national story is for ever evolving and the very notion of 'a nation' has more the connotations of an organism than a fixture, with a life of its own. As described by Christopher Harding, in a book about Japan:

---

[1] Rotberg, R., ed. (2006) *Israeli and Palestinian Narratives of Conflict: History's Double Helix* Bloomington & Indianapolis, Indiana University Press, p.23.

[2] Cohen, A. (2017) 'Israel's civic education wars: a review of the literature and theoretical implications' *Educational Review*, DOI: 10.1080/00131911.2017.1407295.

[3] See Brand, L. (2014) *Politics and National Narratives: Official Stories, Egypt and Algeria* Stanford: Stanford University Press.

A good story offers purchase on life. It helps herd the happenings and anxieties of past, present and future into some coherent, meaningful whole. But cherished stories can become so powerful that people suffer serving them – and suffer too, if forced to probe or part with them. And though a story may give shape to a single life or nation, it risks doing so at the cost of a steady loss of the ability to see, think and imagine otherwise – about one's self or one's home.[4]

As this depiction encapsulates, a national story has qualities akin to religious belief, such that it is not easily relinquished when challenged by others. Its believers may even contemplate or justify death in its name. Similarly also, we learn about a religion through stories. To elaborate my point here, I can offer an anecdote from the Olive Tree experience. I remember an occurrence which took place at one of the public forums I convened about some or other aspect of the Israeli-Palestinian conflict, when many of the Olive Tree participants were present in the audience. These participants let out a collective gasp when an outsider to the programme asked the question: 'Why can't you agree to set aside your respective narratives and simply address the facts and move on?'

What this person was effectively asking was: 'Why can't you all forget who you are and what has made you who you are, and simply agree to get along?' That person failed to understand that the coexistence of contradictory narratives *is* the reality. This way of understanding the conflict was one of the insights which Damian Gorman brought to the Olive Tree from his experience in Northern Ireland. The stories and experiences of members of the Protestant community do not negate those of the Catholic community and vice versa. They are both *real* and lived daily by the protagonists, and for many of the Olive Tree participants this way of understanding things made sense, once they had been through the experience of researching and presenting their respective mainstream national narratives to each other (as described in Chapter 2).

However, most people are not exposed to an exercise such as this and most people are not lifted out of their respective communities, flown to a far-away city and deposited in a university alongside other students from around the world, including the people they have learnt to see as their enemies, and invited

---

[4] Harding, C. (2018) *Japan Story: In Search of a Nation, 1850 to the Present* London: Allen Lane, p.4.

to compare stories. On the contrary, the norm for most people is that they grow up learning only their own story and when told about another one, will dismiss it as biased and non-factual.

This is not to say that facts do not exist, nor that the contrasting narratives are invented or pure make-believe. In the words of Michel-Rolph Trouillot, 'not any fiction can pass for history'.[5] He made this point in a book he wrote about the history of Haiti and how Europeans in the eighteenth and nineteenth centuries could not grasp what Haitians themselves knew about their history because, in the European view of the world, the notion of a revolution mounted successfully by black slaves against their white masters was inconceivable. Instead, in the European worldview of the time: 'Blacks were inferior and therefore enslaved; black slaves behaved badly and were therefore inferior',[6] and thence incapable of acting in a manner that white Europeans could.

Even if not pure fiction, however, national narratives *are* constructed in the sense that they include some 'facts' but not others, some people or groups, but not others, and they assign meaning, significance, motives and values to the events and actors they feature. As the familiar dictum has it, the history we are exposed to in our school textbooks and popular movies is usually the one preferred and written by the victors not the vanquished. Thus, the way imperial powers wrote about the people they colonised habitually depicted them as less 'civilized' and less 'developed' than themselves.

Such depictions enabled the imperialists to justify colonization as a benign, civilizing mission. In her work on the British in Mandate Palestine, Zeina Ghandour documents the way in which British colonial officers operated on the ground. The tools they used to exercise control included not only military force but also bureaucratic procedures, 'scientific' assessments and legal instruments – to establish and regulate land ownership and agricultural production. The goal, according to British official records, was to completely overhaul – and thereby 'improve' – the existing way of life. And in pursuit of this mission, British civil servants saw themselves as morally ennobling the natives and themselves.

They advertised and wrote about their missions in terms of devotion and

---

[5] Trouillot, M. (1995) *Silencing the Past: Power and the Production of History* Boston: Beacon Press, p.29.

[6] Ibid, p.77.

sacrifice, progress and humanity, honour and bravery. A veil of benevolence and self-effacement sheathed the individual actions of these imperial agents. They saw themselves as servants of a higher cause, and their master was not only the British Government, or the King, or God, but humanity and civilization.[7]

In her work Ghandour also discusses the absence of Arab records and accounts of their experiences at the hands of the British Mandatory authorities. To redress this imbalance, she recorded many oral testimonies of Palestinians who lived under the Mandate or were told about it by their parents, and presents these in her analysis.

For the historical 'facts' we rely on records – of births, deaths, and injuries – texts of speeches, diaries, official pronouncements and censuses, monuments, buildings, and ruins. As a consequence, the telling of history requires both archives and access to archives, and a complaint commonly voiced by Palestinian historians has been that many of the books and records collected by Palestinians living in Mandate Palestine were destroyed or confiscated during the 1948 war.[8] Others were lost in the war of 1967 or disappeared during the Israeli invasion of Beirut in 1982 and the 'reinvasion' of Palestinian population centres in the West Bank in 2002.

On the Israeli side, a group who became known as 'the new historians' gained notoriety in the 1980s when their research in Israeli archives found documentary evidence which undermined the Israeli 'official narrative' that the Palestinians had 'chosen' to abandon their homes in 1948. In any case, the significance of what they found or failed to find is disputed even among the new historians. Thus there is no single 'objective' history of the Israelis and the Palestinians against which to judge the veracity of the national narratives they

---

[7] Ghandour, Z. (2010) *A Discourse on Domination in Mandate Palestine: Imperialism, Property and Insurgency* Oxford: Routledge, p.16. Inspired by Ghandour's book, I invited her to meet some of the Olive Tree students. They were fascinated by her insights on the British and because she introduced herself as Lebanese-British and a scholar of law she was welcomed by them as unusual in her interest in aspects of their story, i.e. she was not one of the many Israeli or Palestinian 'experts' on the conflict, though when she admitted to partial Palestinian heritage, some sighed a little.

[8] See Khalidi, R. (1997) *Palestinian Identity: the Construction of Modern National Consciousness* New York: Columbia University Press.

each espouse. The reality is the coexistence of various and competing narratives which cannot be reconciled into one single 'bridging narrative'.[9]

As the victors in post-Mandate Palestine, the Israelis have had various advantages, in the battle of the narratives. These advantages derive from the attributes of statehood and leadership awareness of the powers accruing to any state authority was evident in the Zionist movement even before the state was won. The leaders of the movement made a conscious effort to forge a new Jewish national identity, replete with its own language (based on ancient Hebrew) and values. Once the state was declared, the Israeli authorities established a national curriculum to be taught in the state school system. This curriculum has since undergone several revisions,[10] but has always and unsurprisingly given precedence to narratives which serve the state rather than its opponents.[11]

Those Palestinians who remained in what became Israel in 1948 found themselves under Israeli military rule initially and not at liberty to choose their own school curricula or explain 'the *Nakba*' in their history books.[12] The Palestinians in the West Bank came under Jordanian rule between 1948 and 1967 and were obliged to use the Jordanian curriculum in their schools. Those who

---

[9] As discussed at length and from contrasting perspectives in Rotberg, R., ed. (2006) *Israeli and Palestinian Narratives of Conflict: History's Double Helix* Bloomington & Indianapolis, Indiana University Press.

[10] For an account of the dilemmas faced in drawing up a curriculum that simultaneously promoted democratic values and national belonging see: Cohen, A. (2017) 'Israel's civic education wars: a review of the literature and theoretical implications' *Educational Review*, DOI: 10.1080/00131911.2017.1407295.

[11] For an account of the versions of Israeli history taught in Israeli schools between 1948 and the early 21st century see Naveh, E. 'The Dynamics of Identity Construction in Israel through Education in History' in Rotberg, R., ed. (2006) *Israeli and Palestinian Narratives of Conflict: History's Double Helix* Bloomington & Indianapolis, Indiana University Press; and for an analysis of how the Palestinians have featured in Israeli school books see: Peled-Elhanan, N. (2012) *Palestine in Israeli School Books: Ideology and Propaganda in Education* London: I.B.Tauris; and Teff-Seker, Y. (2016) *Palestinians in Israeli Textbooks* Impact-se Report Update, www.impact-se. org/wp-content/uploads/Palestinians-in-Israeli_Textbooks_2016-Update.pdf.

[12] By the end of the twentieth century, it was possible to discuss the *Nakba* in the schools, though the way the term is explained has remained a subject of contention. One of the Olive Tree students, a Palestinian citizen of Israel, made a study of the role of collective memory and narrative in the construction of identity among Palestinians in Israel for her final year undergraduate dissertation at City, University of London. In this she reflected on the version of her own history that she was permitted to learn in school and how that compared with what her family told her.

ended up in the Gaza Strip after 1948 came under Egyptian administration and had to use Egyptian textbooks in their schools. These arrangements were maintained by the Israelis after they occupied the West Bank and Gaza in the war of 1967.

Thus, it was not until the 1990s and the establishment of the Palestinian Authority (PA) following the Oslo Accords that the Palestinians were permitted to write their own schoolbooks. Even then, aware that they were under close scrutiny by the international donors and the Israelis, in this and every other aspect of their administration, the PA initially sanctioned only a very circumscribed version of the Palestinian story in the first new schoolbooks. These made little if any mention of the Israelis, apart from oblique references to soldiers; omitted details of the Oslo Accords; and provided no clear indication of the borders of Palestine.

According to Nathan Brown, who made a detailed study of the books in 2001,[13] and published other analyses on the subject, they were 'more remarkable for their omissions than for their content' and 'show dedication to the principle that national identity depends on loyalty to authority and that different sources of authority – family, locality, nation, religion, and humanity – are not merely harmonious but almost identical'.[14] In response to claims made by Israeli critics that Palestinian school books taught hatred of Israeli Jews, Brown countered that such assertions were based on the contents of Egyptian and Jordanian texts used in the past and that:

> Palestinian schools do not teach hate through their books, but they cannot teach children how to accomplish what has eluded adults, which is to resolve the issues that have bedevilled Palestinians since before 1948.[15]

Following the introduction of a new PA curriculum in 2016-17, new criticisms were levelled at the PA over the content of the new textbooks, with the Jerusalem-based Institute for Monitoring Peace and Cultural Tolerance in

---

[13] Brown, N. (2001) *Democracy, History, and the Contest over the Palestinian Curriculum* Report prepared for the Adam Institute.

[14] Brown, N. (2006) 'Contesting National Identity in Palestinian Education' in Rotberg, R., ed. (2006) *Israeli and Palestinian Narratives of Conflict*, p.241.

[15] Ibid.

School Education (IMPACT-se) asserting:

> new curriculum deliberately omits any discussion of peace education or reference to any Jewish presence in Palestine before1948. Most troubling, there is a systematic insertion of violence, martyrdom and jihad across all grades and subjects in a more extensive and sophisticated manner, embracing a full spectrum of extreme nationalist ideas and Islamist ideologies that extend even into the teaching of science and mathematics.[16]

This and other such claims prompted the EU (the main funder of the PA) to instigate its own study of Palestinian textbooks. As this illustrates, the matter of school curricula remains a site of vigorous political contestation – it is one of the many battlegrounds in the conflict.

Following Israeli independence, the institution of the military – the Israel Defence Forces or IDF – became a central component in the building of Israeli national belonging. All Jewish Israelis (excluding the Ultra Orthodox) are expected to serve in the IDF, or perform some other form of national service, unless they claim or are given exemption on grounds of conscience or disability. To my knowledge only a couple of Jewish Israelis awarded Olive Tree scholarships had sought such exemption, and as they described, they knew in so doing they were choosing to forego the kind of social approbation and potential career advantages accorded to their peers who did serve. Palestinians, including Palestinian citizens of Israel, have no equivalent to this institutional induction into the national group identity.

What many Palestinians do have, by contrast, are the attributes of refugee status. Those Palestinians who fled or were expelled from their homes in 1947-8 ended up in refugee camps, some in the Gaza Strip and the West Bank and others in Lebanon, Syria and Jordan. They were registered by the United Nations as refugees and that status was also accorded to their children and grandchildren, even if the latter did not dwell in camps any more. The camps were administered by a dedicated UN body called the UN Relief and Works Agency (UNRWA), and it continues to provide education for refugee children and food aid for refugee families who cannot provide for themselves.

---

[16] See: www.impact-se.org/wp-content/uploads/PA-Reports_-Combined-Selected-Examples. pdf

The status of Palestinian refugees in Lebanon, Syria and Jordan excludes them from full citizenship in those countries, though their exact circumstances vary and in Jordan they have passports, albeit not on a par with those of other Jordanians. Palestinians living in the West Bank and Gaza, whether registered refugees or not, also have no citizenship of a state. Since the mid-1990s, they can apply for passports issued by the PA in Ramallah – but these do not accord them the protection of a state. Palestinian ID cards, printed in Arabic and Hebrew, are registered with the Israeli authorities.

The Israelis have long maintained that it should be up to the governments of the Arab host countries to integrate those Palestinian refugees who live in their states. However, these governments have chosen not to do so, pending an agreed resolution of the Israeli-Palestinian conflict. In the absence of such a deal, refugee status remains the official identity of many hundreds of thousands of Palestinians.

As I discovered in the course of a project on the Palestinian refugee issue that I ran with a Lebanese colleague at Chatham House between the late 1990s and early 2000s, many of the refugees living outside what became the Occupied Territories in 1967 (the West Bank and Gaza) perceived the Oslo Accords as portending their eternal exile from their historical homeland. As they explained to their counterparts from inside the West Bank and Gaza, the fact of their refugee status entitled them to priority consideration in any peace deal. They wanted 'the right of return' and compensation in accordance with UN Resolution 194 of 1948.

In other words, the dominant national narrative of many Palestinians is a story of becoming refugees or exiles from the land of their parents or grandparents and to be without citizenship of anywhere. For them, to be a Palestinian is to be descended from the refugees of 1947-8. This applied to those Olive Tree participants who grew up in refugee camps in the West Bank and Gaza Strip, all of whom could name the village or town in Israel from which their parents or grandparents originated. If you asked them where they were from, they would usually ask whether you meant 'originally' or more immediately. Their formal identification is thus derivative of the conflict.

Palestinians brought up in camps near to or inside the main Palestinian towns of Gaza, Nablus, Ramallah or Bethlehem describe being looked upon with suspicion by the town residents and seen as potential troublemakers. Their way of dealing with this quite often has been to own their refugee status as a badge of authenticity. They may describe the ethos of life in the camp – the deprivations, the poverty, the night raids by the Israeli soldiers – with a kind of stoic pride. Such is the stuff of group narratives and, as in any society, the subtext of the narratives reveals the existence of sub-categories or classes within 'the nation'.

Particularly revealing was the way Olive Tree Palestinians from the West Bank or Gaza, refugee or non-refugee, regarded those Palestinians who grew up in Israel. Even if some of these families had been 'internally displaced' in 1948, the sense prevailed that they had sold out or abandoned the Palestinian cause. As a result, the Palestinian citizens of Israel tried to set the record straight, as they saw it, by explaining that their families had simply managed to avoid expulsion, had experienced discrimination and identified as Palestinian.

In any case, without the attributes of sovereignty, including their own armed forces, and given that most of them are scattered around the region, the Palestinians cannot expect to match the Israelis in the coherence, cohesion, self-confidence and sophistication of their national identity and national narrative. In fact, the Palestinian narrative is in many respects derivative of, or reactive to, the Israeli one. According to Saleh Abdel Jawad:

> Arab historians obviously contest the mythical elements of the Israeli accounts. But these historians nevertheless sometimes remain trapped in Israeli paradigms.[17]

An illustration of this problem was evident in the responses of Palestinians to my question about their identity, as recounted in the previous chapter. Several felt it necessary to assert a derivation from the Canaanites, which would mean their ancestors were already on the land when the Jews first arrived, in Biblical times, and by implication, therefore, have precedence in that land.

When Palestinians use the building blocks of the Israeli national narrative, as the bases for their own story, they reveal not only their own defensiveness but also the way the narratives have become inextricably interlinked, as well as totally different. The Israelis have set the pace and they have a state, while the vast majority of Palestinians are left stateless. During Olive Tree discussions I sensed that the Israelis *and* the Palestinians saw more *strength*, though not

---

[17] Abdel Jawad, S. (2006) 'The Arab and Palestinian Narratives of the 1948 War' in Rotberg, ed. (2006) *Israeli and Palestinian Narratives of Conflict*, p.79.

legitimacy, in the Israeli narrative than in the Palestinian one. The Palestinians therefore face a struggle to present themselves as more substantial than simply 'the losers', especially when they lack the institutions of statehood and the endorsement of international recognition with which to do so.

The Israelis have a different problem with their national narrative. No one story covers all. The Zionist version of the national story that reflected the vision of the predominantly Ashkenazy elite that founded the state could not last beyond the 1960s. The arrival of Jewish migrants from across the Arab world, the occupation of the West Bank and Gaza Strip, inclusive of their Palestinian inhabitants, the ingathering of Ethiopian Jews, and the immigration of around a million Russian Jews in the 1990s, changed the demographics and diversified the culture. National religious and Orthodox agendas challenged the predominantly secularist old order. With time came a growing realisation that 'Israel's historic narrative can no longer be taught as one story and one memory, but only as a mosaic of intercommunicating stories and memories.'[18] Thus, even if the state seeks to control the narrative, there are limits to its capacity.

In the specific case of the Israelis and Palestinians there is another very important factor to take into account in this analysis. The conflict between these two peoples has been in progress for so long now that few if any of those born and brought up in the land they both claim as their own can have experienced life *without* the conflict. The conflict *is* their life, in many ways, and their life-story is inseparable from the history of the conflict. As a result, the national narratives of both the Palestinians and the Israelis – the stories which define them, their origins, struggles, victories, and defeats – are also their 'conflict narratives'.

It is of course the case that both communities do not define themselves *only* in relation to one another. Jewish Israelis distinguish themselves from diaspora Jews and Palestinians distinguish themselves from other Arabs. However, even when they do this, it is the conflict which makes them different. Jewish Israelis depict themselves as living under siege in a hostile neighbourhood and bearing the burden – risking 'the ultimate sacrifice' – in defending their state and thence a safe haven for all Jews, in a way that Jews living elsewhere are expected to acknowledge and support. Palestinians explain themselves as either living in exile

---

[18] Naveh, E. (2006) 'The Dynamics of Identity Construction in Israel through Education in History' in Rotberg, ed. (2006) *Israeli and Palestinian Narratives of Conflict*, p.268.

from their homeland, most of them unable to even visit it, or else living under occupation (or siege in the case of Gaza) or struggling for equal rights inside Israel.

Some analysts of the Israeli-Palestinian conflict define it as 'an intractable conflict'.[19] However, in doing so they do not explain whether the intractability of the conflict derives from the conflicting narratives or vice versa. Alternatively, there are those who describe the relationship between the narratives and the conflict as dialectic, rather than linear.[20] This conceptualisation comes close to what I discern, but I remain sceptical about the value of trying to define the sequencing at all, because I cannot see either narrative distinct from the conflict at any point in the last hundred years or so, and certainly not in the consciousness and stories of the two collective identities. The national narratives are also conflict narratives and it makes no sense to me to assert that there are conflict issues separate from narrative issues, or that while the former can be resolved, the latter are less amenable to resolution.

The national narratives are inextricable from the conflict *and* from each other. Further, one narrative is the story of the winner and the other is the story of the loser. One party is in overall control of the other and, in that sense, they are not equal and their narratives give voice to an unequal situation. The conflict persists so long as the protagonists act out their unequal parts in the drama. They are both trapped in their narratives and it is in this sense that I define the narratives as drivers. It is possible for individuals to extricate themselves from a slavish commitment to the compulsions of their national narrative and identity – and escape the 'narrative trap'. Yet to attain that level of individual agency requires both the opportunity and the courage to dissociate from the prevailing norms.

The Olive Tree programme presented an opportunity for some of the participants at least to make such a leap. As described in Chapter 2, those involved were enjoined to research their respective national narratives of the conflict and

---

[19] See in particular, Bar-Tal, D. and Gavriel Salomon (2006) 'Israeli-Jewish Narratives of the Israeli-Palestinian Conflict: Evolution, Contents, Functions, and Consequences' in Rotberg, ed. (2006) *Israeli and Palestinian Narratives of Conflict*, p.20.

[20] Bar-On, D. and Sami Adwan (2006) 'The Psychology of Better Dialogue between Two Separate but Interdependent Narratives' in Rotberg, ed. (2006) *Israeli and Palestinian Narratives of Conflict*.

to present their findings to the rest of the group. They were encouraged to re-read their school textbooks, look up TV documentaries, and interview friends and family members to arrive at a broad outline of their respective narratives of key events. They were not asked to present their own personal theories and stories about those events. In the process of narrating one national history and listening to a narration of the other, they could not avoid noticing the emotional power of each narrative. They could see how each of them embodied within it their respective national identities.

Crucially, it began to dawn on everyone, myself included, that to ask someone to relinquish or fundamentally revise their own narrative is to ask them to reconsider their own identity. That is a very big ask – it is undermining, disorientating and potentially alarming. Hence the necessity for the facilitators of any cross-conflict dialogue exercise to understand the enormity of what is at stake for the participants if they dig deep enough to come to grips with the core elements in the conflict. It is not just about which and how much territory is in dispute, which is no small thing in itself, but is also, fundamentally, about identity.

In contrast to the exercise just described, the narratives discussed below are not the official ones approved by the Israeli state or the Palestinian Authority and taught in their respective schools. They are the narratives voiced by the individuals whom I surveyed for this study. Of central interest here is not how the Israeli or Palestinian leaderships recount their respective national stories, but how these have been internalized by members of the two communities.

As explained previously, the survey respondents quoted here could in no way be considered representative samples of their respective societies, but the groups surveyed were comparable with one another, as explained in Chapter 2 and I refer the reader to that chapter, pages 48-51, for the specific details and necessary caveats.

Israeli Perspectives on the Starting Point of the Conflict

When posed the question 'How far back – to what date/era do we need to go to identify the origins of the conflict?' most Israeli respondents, both Olive Tree and non-Olive Tree, identified the origins as dating back to the late 19th or early

20th century, the foundation of the Zionist movement and the first or second Aliya (Jewish migrations) to 'the land of Israel' or 'Eretz Israel'. The exceptions to this general pattern dated the origins back to Biblical times – whether as a precursor to the contemporary conflict or as a statement of the age-old Jewish experience.

Some respondents singled out the Balfour Declaration as a key milestone in the genesis of the conflict – a 'point of no return'. Most of them also depicted Jewish 'settlement of the land' as meeting with Arab hostility.

Here are some examples:

Three non-Olive Tree Israeli Responses
1. The period of the Second Aliya (the first decade of the 20th century).

2. I think that there are two different time periods that can be pointed out in order to identify the origins of the conflict. We can go back to ancient times – biblical times – when the Israelites walked 40 years in the desert, reached the land of Israel (Eretz Israel) – the land of the forefathers – settled in Israel, established Jerusalem as Israel's capital and so on. This ancient period, and the origins of the Jewish people, give the people of Israel the 'legitimacy' and the 'right' to this piece of land. Back then there were already fights with the Philistines (or the Palestinians of our days) who 'stood up against us to destroy us' (for example, the story of Delilah, the Philistine, who cut off Samson the Hero's hair – which was the source of his strength). From this period we can already learn that the Jews were a haunted people [*as in endangered or hunted – translator's note*]. For example, in the story of Masada – who had to fight for their own existence against all other non-Jewish people (see for example the phrase 'pour out thy wrath upon the nations' from the Passover Haggadah). Perhaps this is where the roots of the conflict lie (we can also go back to the Book of Genesis biblical story of Jacob and Esau). However, it is more popular, and I think it is more fitting, to view the origins of the conflict in 1948 with the establishment of the state of Israel, when the Arab residents of this land opposed this move, which was approved by the United Nations. This decision of the UN led to a war (the War of Independence).

3. As the waves of Aliya to Palestine, or 'West of the Jordan Eretz Israel' (a name given to this piece of land by the Jews of the Aliya from Eastern Europe in the 19th century), accelerated, frictions began to take place between the different populations, which were different by religion from each other. That is, frictions between Jews and non-Jews (especially Muslims). These frictions took place in the 'job market', i.e. on the backdrop of the struggle over jobs and livelihood (a conflict between the Jews of the 'New Yishuv' and the cheap Arab labourers). The conflict between these two populations in the job market deepened the overall conflict between these groups and consolidated the Arabs, who lived here before 1882, as Arab-Palestinians or, in short, as Palestinians with a defined national identity. In other words, an identity, linking the Arab population (which was mostly Muslim, with a Christian minority) to the piece of land where they reside, was formed and given a name – Palestinian. Therefore, we have to go back to the end of the 19th century in order to put a date for the origins of this conflict. In order to identify the roots of the conflict we must focus on the struggle that took place in the job market in Palestine/Eretz Israel during that time period, a struggle which gave birth to, and signified, two distinct groups – Jewish and Palestinian – as hawkish national groups.

Three Israeli Olive Tree Alumni Responses

1. It is difficult for me to answer this question: from the Jewish/Israeli angle, I feel that it is important to talk about biblical times in order to explain the affiliation of the Jewish people to Israel. On the other hand, the biblical context is not really relevant to many Israelis, and it is not relevant at all to Palestinians. Therefore, it may be best to start at the end of the 19th century with the beginning of Zionism.

2. This is the question I ask those who ask me who is to blame for the conflict. In fact, by stating this or that date, we are basically asking to point a finger at 'the one who started it' [*the conflict*]. Therefore, I cannot ignore the fact that determining a specific date or an historical time period is in itself part of those identities which are in conflict. Thus, my opinion is that [*by answering this question*] I am contributing to the cycle of blame and therefore to the continuation of the conflict.

Hence, my official response is that we shouldn't go back in time and instead focus on the achievements which were accomplished so far in the direction of conversations [*between Israelis and Palestinians*] and of resolving the conflict, while also focusing on mediation between the different identities. However, the roots of the conflict are significant for understanding these identities and for mediating between them. If I was asked this question before I was exposed to the other side of the conflict, my answer would be the events of 1921 [*the Jaffa Riots*] and of 1929 [*the 1929 Palestine Riots*], events which strengthen the claim that my side isn't the one that started [*the conflict*]. Today I believe that the roots of the conflict lie in the approval given to the Jewish people in the Balfour Declaration to establish a national home in Israel. This was an official certificate of approval which threatened the people, and/or the ethnic group, that lived in the area.

3. We need to go back to the beginning of the 20th century, to the '20s and '30s of the twentieth century, when the Arabs understood that the aspiration for establishing a Jewish State in the land of Israel [*Eretz Israel*] puts their future sovereignty in the area, and the characteristics of the land, under jeopardy. Jewish-Arab relations in the area were not always bad. It was the national aspirations of both people that changed the picture.

As these examples illustrate, Olive Tree Israelis demonstrated awareness of the potentially negative implications for peace-building of assigning blame and were reluctant to play that game. Two alumni dated the origins to Biblical times – the rest to the late 19th or early 20th centuries, but they were generally reluctant to single out one date and instead saw the conflict as a series of 'layers'.

Yet in all the Israeli responses the message was fairly clear – the Jewish migrants to Eretz Israel did not come looking for a fight but they encountered hostility. Most respondents made reference to hostility from, and clashes with, the Arabs, whether in the 1920s or on the establishment of the state of Israel in 1948. One noted that the clashes of 1922 were the origin of a Palestinian national identity and thence a conflict between two identities.

The non-Olive Tree respondents also emphasised the fact that the early Zionists chose to till their own land, rather than use cheaper local labourers, as a key source of the hostility. As such, they discerned a socio-economic dimension to the original conflict, and one respondent referenced a Zionist 'desire to alter the character of the country' as the problem. Yet the same respondents also referred to religious differences as explanation for clashes with the Arabs. For many of them the hostile reception encountered by the Jewish migrants was a replay of their experience elsewhere and in Biblical times, the habitual fate of the Jews.

Overall, the prevailing view among the Israeli respondents, both Olive Tree and non-Olive Tree, was that the conflict originated with the hostile Arab reaction to the arrival of Jewish migrants in the historical land of Israel and/or the foundation of the Jewish state. They did not depict the migrations as an occupation or refer to the post-1967 occupation of the West Bank and Gaza. Instead, they saw their Jewish migrant forebears as the ones experiencing a hostile reception from the locals and thereby obliged to fight for their survival. The Zionist project – the Jewish state – was thus established in a hostile environment, it was born in conflict.

Israeli Views on the Origins of the Conflict

In respondents' answers to the question 'What are the origins of the conflict?' two main themes emerged. The dominant one was that the conflict derives from two competing national claims to the same land (and holy sites) and/or the emergence of two national movements. A refinement to this was the view that the Jewish national awakening preceded and prompted Palestinian national awakening. One respondent repeated the view that 'non-Jewish' hostility to competition for labouring jobs was a contributory cause of conflict.

The less dominant theme related the origins of the conflict to European anti-Semitism and the Holocaust, leaving the Jews with no choice but Israel for their survival – forcing the Palestinians 'to pay the price' and creating a 'zero-sum game'. One respondent blamed 'the representation of European Aliya Jews as a "foreign element" in the area as an expression of Arab nationalism'.

Another respondent saw the origins of the conflict in the UN Partition Plan and recognition of the Jewish claim to statehood; while another saw the 1967 war and Israeli occupation of the West Bank and Gaza Strip as the origins of the conflict.

Here are some examples.

Three non-Olive Tree Israeli Responses

1. I think that the origins of the conflict, as we experience it today, lie in the UN's Partition Plan that divided the land into two states for two people – a plan that the Jews accepted and celebrated, as it meant the ratification of the state of Israel for the Jewish people. For the Arab residents of the area this plan constituted a disaster (Nakba), manifested in the theft of their lands. Another significant milestone for understanding the conflict as it exists today is the Six Day War of 1967 which ended with Israel occupying the Palestinian territories and establishing military rule in these areas, which significantly affects the daily lives of the Palestinian population living in those areas.

2. On the one hand, there was the Jewish national awakening, which led to Jews settling in Eretz Israel starting from the end of the 19th century. On the other hand, there was the Palestinian national awakening, which led to the failed struggle against the Jewish settlements, and, after the establishment of the state, against the state of Israel. The Palestinian awakening took place after the Jewish awakening and the Palestinian struggle against the Jewish national movement began too late. In light of this, the struggle's ability to make significant gains was limited and it failed to achieve its most significant objective – the establishment of a [*Palestinian*] nation state.

3. The Balfour Declaration, in fact, distilled the origins of the conflict, which are the true tragedy in this story – both sides are actually right: the Jewish people have no other solution, apart from Eretz Israel, for surviving anti-Semitism (following the strengthening of this phenomenon in Eastern Europe at the end of the 19th century, and as was, in retrospect, proven in the Holocaust), and, in parallel, the Palestinians are the ones who have to 'pay' the price for the Jewish problem with their land, against their own wishes. This basic clash of interests (between the two sides) is the root of the conflict, with both sides thinking they are right and, by so doing, cancelling the justifications of the other side. A zero-sum game.

Three Israeli Olive Tree Alumni Responses

1. The origins of the conflict lie in the lack of compatibility between the Israeli and Palestinian national aspirations. With the rise of nation states worldwide, the Israelis and Palestinians also wanted to establish a nation state [*of their own*] in the territory of Mandate Palestine. The Palestinians believed that the territory belonged to them because they were always there. The Jews believed that the territory belongs to them because this is what the Bible says. In addition, many of them, like my grandmother and grandfather, thought the land was empty and that they were not stealing anyone's land. This is what the leaders told them.

2. Zionism is an expression of European nationalism. There is no possibility to realise peace in the Middle East as long as Zionism, in its modern state, represents such a traditional type of nationalism and as long as it is so aggressive to anyone who is not Jewish. Palestinian nationalism, which has been shaped according to the appearance and characteristics of Israeli nationalism, may be just as extreme.

3. A clash between national identities. The modern national ideas, as they spread around Europe during the 19th century, also spread beyond the borders of Europe following the collapse of empires during the First World War. The Zionist movement, as the representative of the Jewish nation in its modern form, versus the beginning of the Arab national movement during the 1920s, and, later on, versus the strengthening of the Palestinian nation. What these identities have in common is the territorial claim over the same territory, and in that, over its holy sites, cultural characteristics etc. But national identities are primarily mutually exclusive, or, in other words, 'what I am not'. Therefore, when a national identity which is different to my own claims the same thing that characterises my own identity, it unsettles the wholeness and the stability of my identity and this leads to conflict.

Among the non-Olive Tree Israeli respondents, the legitimacy of the Israeli/Jewish national claim appeared unquestioned – with varying levels of recognition that this is contested by others. In contrast, the Olive Tree alumni conveyed less automatic identification with the legitimacy of the Israeli claim and greater appreciation of the Palestinian situation.

The Israeli alumni did not mention '67 or the Partition Plan or the Holocaust in identifying the origins. They chimed with the depiction of two competing national movements and claims, but in a more detached way, referring to 'national aspirations' for statehood and with one noting that Palestinian claims are based on the belief that they were always there. One, quoted above, reported that the Jewish claim was based on what the Bible says and the fact that they were told the land was 'empty'.

Variations on the language used by the non-Olive Tree Israeli respondents included mention of: a colonialist movement versus the indigenous population; 'exclusive identities'; the effects of 'British colonialism' on nationalist sentiment; and the Palestinians' response to 'the threat' of Israeli nationalism. One respondent said that the *Nakba* shaped Palestinian identity.

The last of the examples quoted above stands out as a vivid illustration of what one Olive Tree alumnus at least had learnt about national identity and competing national narratives through dialogue with the Palestinians. The response of another Olive Tree alumnus indicated an appreciation that the Arabs were provoked as well as hostile. He/she defined the origins of the conflict thus:

> The consolidation of the Zionist movement and the beginning of the Jewish immigration to Palestine, the attempts to establish a Jewish state in Palestine and the threat that the Palestinians felt in light of these attempts.

Overall, and as will become clear below, Jewish Israeli alumni proved more willing to recognize what they had learned, whereas the Palestinians appeared to lack the confidence to do that. That said, my observation is that the Israelis arrived in London with more confidence in the first place.

Palestinian Perspectives on the Starting Point of the Conflict

When asked: 'How far back – to what date/era do we need to go to identify the origins of the conflict?' Palestinian respondents had a range of views. Somewhat surprisingly, to me, several non-Olive Tree respondents thought that the Oslo Agreement was the starting point for the contemporary conflict, because 'that was when the compromises started' and the situation deteriorated for the Palestinians. They blamed their own side for going along with it.

By contrast, a number of other non-Olive Tree respondents saw the end of the Caliphate and partitioning of the Levant (Sykes-Picot and the Balfour Declaration were mentioned) in World War I as marking the start of the conflict. These developments allowed the entry of Jews and occupation, and 'gave the land to those who didn't have the right and displaced the true owners of the land'. One respondent said Jewish immigration predated Balfour, while during the British Mandate 'they started to take our land'. Another identified 1897 and the first Zionist Congress as the start of the conflict.

Another view was that 1948 and the *Nakba* started a chain of events, compounded in 1967 with the *Naksa*.

Intersecting the various other views, one respondent explained that the conflict had existed for a long time but 'the wall' and the settlements made it worse. Another elaborated on this with a list: oppression – check points, settlements and the apartheid wall – and concluded 'every day the problems increase'.

In direct opposition to the general Israeli view that it was not the Jewish migrants who instigated the conflict, the prevailing Palestinian view was that hostile and oppressive measures taken against them were what started the conflict. Here are some examples of Palestinian perspectives on the starting point of the conflict:

Three non-Olive Tree Palestinian Responses

1. Oslo Agreement. Because when we signed Oslo the compromises started. The situation started getting worse. It all started with Oslo.

2. I think before the Balfour Declaration. We can say from that period. That's when Jewish immigration started. During the British Mandate Jewish immigration and infiltrating started. And they started to take our land.

3. In my opinion the Palestinian people passed through many junctures all of which have paved the way for the Israeli occupation. Even before Balfour all the events that took place were planned and paved the way to create a homeland for the Jews in Palestine. I think the Palestinian situation was good with the resistance until 1993-1994 when Oslo was signed. After that there were negotiations which took a different course. We made a lot of compromises.

Three Palestinian Olive Tree Alumni Responses

1. I think we need to go back to 1917 to identify the causes of the conflict. We can also go back even further to the establishment of the Zionist movement.

2. We need to go back to the Zionist ambitions for the land of Palestine that started at the end of the 19th century. These ambitions form the real start of the Palestinian-Israeli conflict. If it wasn't for these ambitions for the land of Palestine the Balfour Declaration wouldn't have been issued and the Jewish immigration to Palestine wouldn't have increased, and the Nakba and the ethnic cleansing of Palestine wouldn't have taken place.

3. In my mind, it is rather irrelevant and, perhaps, counterproductive to try and go back to a certain time(s) or event(s) in order to identify the roots of the conflict. However, for me as a Palestinian, the British Mandate of Palestine can be considered as the time period that can, roughly, indicate the recent conflict but the real causes of this conflict are well rooted in the history of both the Arabs and the Jewish people, but also the troubled part of the world called the "Holy Land."

That several of the non-Olive Tree Palestinian respondents cited the Oslo Accords as the starting point for the current conflict says to me that the everyday experience of those respondents – all Palestinians living in the Occupied Territories – was uppermost in their minds. As they saw it the creation of the Palestinian Authority (PA), along with its own police force, had ended all-out Palestinian resistance to Israeli occupation and placed them under two layers of 'oppression'.

The responses of the Palestinian Olive Tree alumni, by contrast, showed less preoccupation with present problems. All but one of these alumni dated the origins of the conflict to the beginning of Jewish immigration to Palestine, across a period that began in the late 19th century with the foundation of the Zionist movement, through 1917 (Balfour) and the British Mandate, to 1948. The one exception was an alumnus who saw 1967 as the beginning of the conflict.

Distinct from the other alumni, the 5th cohort Palestinians described the conflict as progressing through successive stages, punctuated by key events and becoming progressively worse. They also made mention of Jewish-Arab relations 2000 years ago, when, they believed, relations were not problematic, yet the period has relevance to the current conflict because it explains the Jewish focus on Palestine as the place to establish their modern state.

This is one of a number of instances wherein it becomes clear that the Palestinian Olive Tree alumni were operating with a narrower focus than the non-Olive Tree Palestinians, specifically on the Israeli-Palestinian dimensions of the conflict rather than a larger (Middle East) picture. Also apparent, as mentioned, was that the non-Olive Tree Palestinians were seemingly much more conscious of the day-to-day realities of the occupation in the West Bank than their counterparts living at a distance in London (and/or coming from Gaza, where the day-to-day aspects are different).

Palestinian Views on the Origins of the Conflict

The Palestinian responses to the question: 'What were the origins of the conflict?' can be roughly grouped under four themes. One characterised Palestine as a fertile land, rich in natural resources and religious holy sites, at the centre of successive civilizations, and geo-strategically well placed to command the region. As such it has become the target of enemies, 'not the Jews but primarily the Zionists and then global imperialism'. It is an area of contestation.

Another theme identified Jewish ambitions to control what to them is 'the Promised Land' according to their religion, as in conflict with 'us' – whose land it is, and which also matters to us in religious terms.

A third theme depicted Palestine as the cockpit of a struggle between the West and the Arabs: 'Our conflict is with America more than it is with Israel'. Western motives were identified as a quest to control the oil and the region, and the West created 'an imaginary enemy, which eventually became a real enemy' to the Arab and Muslim regions. Some respondents saw the West as creating both Israel and IS (the Islamic state group) – to stop the true Islam from ruling and flourishing.

A fourth theme had at its centre World War II and 'the charade of the Holocaust' as the events which explain the Jews' need for a country. This was not the only time the term 'charade' was linked to the Holocaust and, as previously noted, this characterisation is fairly common among Palestinians. In the context of the survey, I am not convinced that those using the term were outright denying that the Holocaust happened – though they could have been – but they were quite possibly, or also, referring to what they see as exploitation of the Ho-locaust as justification not only for the Israeli state but also for the cost borne by the Palestinians. Olive Tree alumni did not use the word 'charade', but made mention of the Holocaust as 'an excuse'. Here are some examples of Palestinian views on the origins of the conflict:

Three non-Olive Tree Palestinian Responses

1. Part of the conflict is an attack on the Arabs by the West. Israel man-aged to control us through the efforts of Britain and the events that followed. They want the land and I think religion plays a bigger part than history and our location. Israel needs to control the land because Israel is not a country and they never had a country. They are scattered all over the world. They want to control the land because of religious and historic reasons.

2. For me the main reason is religious. This is their strongest reason to build a country here. Palestine is a country that witnessed many civil-isations such as the Turkish civilisation. With a country with so many civilisations it would be easy to convince people that they were once here. I think this is the strongest reason.

3. I don't understand the question, as it has two sides. On the one hand there is why Palestine and, on the other, there is what are the reasons for the conflict. Why Palestine because, as said by others, the geographic location and because it was part of the Zionist plan. Palestine is the beginning according to their plan. Like others said there are geograph-ic, religious and economic reasons. What is the main reason for the conflict or why did the problems start? They started because of the oc-cupation and the settlements. They wanted to displace us and take the land and that is why it started.

Three Palestinian Olive Tree Alumni Responses

1. Jewish settlement in Palestine and the expulsion of the original inhabi-tants and stealing their land. I want to clarify that this is not a religious conflict. The religion of the settler is irrelevant. If someone steals a land

a conflict will happen irrespective of the settlers' religion or nationality.

2. The conflict is an existential conflict over land and existence at the same time. The Jewish state's attempt to discredit the Palestinian existence on their own land, displace them and take over the land for economic and political reasons related to dominance and maintaining the Zionist entity and the Israeli state.

3. The lack of social and human justice. The poor quality of life that Palestinians live in. Lack of basic freedoms (e.g. freedom of movement, freedom of trade, freedom of economy). The system that Israel has created to protect themselves is paid for by innocent Palestinians who try to get on with their daily lives, making it unbearable and impossible to continue living without reacting towards these difficulties. There's an unlimited number of reasons why the conflict exists and most of it is due to Israeli oppression and the apartheid system they have created whether voluntary or involuntary.

The attribution of the causes of the conflict specifically to the Oslo Accords was unique to members of the 'comparator group' (i.e. non-Olive Tree respondents) and not replicated in the responses of Olive Tree Palestinians. Yet the alumni did attribute the conflict to 'occupation, inequality and racism'; 'oppression and apartheid'; and a string of charges including: forcing the Palestinians to leave their homes; colonization; killings, violence, and deprivation of Palestinian rights. Elaborations on these charges included latter day 'indiscriminate killing and shelling in the Gaza wars' and an imbalance of power between the protagonists, plus 'revenge from both sides'.

One Palestinian alumnus attributed the conflict to: 'The success of the Zionist project in displacing most of the Palestinian people from their land and creating the Jewish state that would solve the Jewish problem at the expense of the original inhabitants of Palestine.'

Some alumni identified the complexities and cross-currents within Israel, between some Israelis and some Palestinians, and between Israel and some Arabs. By way of illustration, according to one alumnus: 'In my opinion, Israel fears peace more because it will increase the social divisions and identity crisis in Israel. It will make the state the enemy of seculars, settlers and the Russians who live on the same land but have nothing in common except the land.'

As this last example suggests, there seemed to be a sophistication to the responses of the alumni compared to those of the non-Olive Tree respondents. There was less if any blame on Western imperialism and Zionist conspiracy and more of a focus on the specifics of the conflict, the cyclical (revenge) aspects, and the imbalance between the parties. As noted, Olive Tree alumni made mention of the Holocaust as 'an excuse' but did not use the term 'the charade of the Holocaust'.

How Views Evolved among Dialogue Participants

In this section, I summarise my findings on the evolution of the views of Israelis and Palestinians in the 5th Cohort, between November 2013 (2 months into their first undergraduate year at City and the Olive Tree experience) and July 2016 (when they had just graduated). As explained in Chapter 2, there were four Jewish Israeli participants in this cohort, two male and two female. There were six Palestinian participants, four men (of whom two came from Gaza, one from the West Bank and one from East Jerusalem) and two women, both Israeli passport-holders.

To arrive at my findings, I compared the answers they gave to the ten questions in November 2013 with those they gave in July 2016.

The 5th Cohort Jewish Israeli Responses

Looking first at the Jewish Israeli responses to the question: 'How far back – to what date/era do we need to go to identify the origins of the conflict? *In the beginning*, in 2013, three out of four dated the origins of the conflict to the late 19th century and the first and second Aliya and the beginning of implementation of the Zionist project. However, one of these elaborated that the origins of the conflict date back to when 'either side's own narrative goes back'; adding, when 'the wave of nationalism swept across the world, Jews and Arabs sought to build a home of their own and realise their wish for self-determination'. The fourth respondent said the crucial start date was 14.5.48, 'the day of the Israeli declaration of independence and the day that the Zionist dream officially became reality'.

At the end, in 2016, the respondents all dated the conflict from the late 19th century and the first and second Aliya, though one noted that 1967 and Oslo also have importance. Another respondent emphasised the period (1920s) when brewing tensions between Arabs and Jews (in Mandate Palestine) first turned into riots and group violence. As encapsulated by a third respondent:

> The origins of the conflict, in its modern constellation, lie at the end of the 19ᵗʰ century, in the period when national movements were created and flourished around Europe and the entire world. During this period, the Zionist Congress in Basel determined that it will act towards the establishment of a Jewish state in the territory of Eretz Israel. From the very moment when this programme began recruiting supporters, and the Jewish Aliya to Palestine began to accelerate, a situation was created in which two people [*nations*] aspire to sovereignty over the same land. This is when the conflict as such began.

My main observation is that whereas in 2013 the main emphasis was placed on when *two* nationalisms clashed; in 2016 there was greater emphasis on the Zionist movement and Jewish nationalism.

Turning to Jewish Israeli views on the origins of the conflict, *in the beginning* the respondents identified nationalism, and the competition between two nationalist movements as at the roots of the conflict, though one did specify: 'As soon as the Zionists identified Palestine, a land already inhabited, as their own "promised land", the conflict started.' Another saw the origins in the Israeli Declaration of Independence.

At the end the respondents were at pains to identify the bases of the competing nationalist claims, with one referring to 'the feelings of belonging' toward the same piece of land of two different peoples, the one based on 'direct, physical connection to the territory of Palestine, which spreads across a few generations' and the other 'based on a historical longing for a Jewish home in Eretz Israel... which became stronger as Jews began suffering from anti-Semitism all around Europe.'

One noted that while Jewish nationalism was infused with the experience of discrimination in Europe, Palestinian nationalism was informed by pan-Arab nationalism and 'the collective experience of the *Nakba*, which shaped Palestinianism as a distinct nation'. Another said: 'The roots of the conflict in my opinion, lie in the radicalisation of the bitterness towards these [Jewish] immigrants whose character was domineering'. And one held the British and religion responsible for the drawing of arbitrary divisions between people.

There was not a pronounced contrast between the 2013 and 2016 responses, except in so far as the latter responses showed even more sensitivity to and acceptance of the other. Notably, there were no judgements as to the relative merits of one or other nationalist movement – in what might be described as a display of magnanimity toward the Palestinian nationalist claims and even a discernment of provocation on the part of the Zionists.

The 5ᵗʰ Cohort Palestinian Responses

When asked 'How far back – to what date/era do we need to go to identify the origins of the conflict?' *in the beginning*, that is in 2013, all the respondents saw the origins as dating from the arrival of Jewish migrants in Palestine and the imperial carve up of the region after World War I. One respondent singled out 1948 as marking the start of dispossession, expulsion, the travails of the refugees and rise of Palestinian nationalism. Two saw fit to explain the importance of going back to the origins because: either, 'Even if we would act differently from our past – we shouldn't ignore what happened'; or, 'It might sound lame, but at least if we are going to make progress to the future at least we should understand "what happened".'

At the end, the responses included more milestones relating to events that drove the Jews to migrate to Palestine, the role of the British Mandate in incubating clashes between them and the Palestinian inhabitants of the land, and a number of subsequent dates marking the progress of the conflict.

The initial responses indicated an aspiration to delve to the bottom of things with a view to making change. The final responses showed much more awareness of the Jewish Israeli narrative. They also conveyed a sense of conflict as a norm or at least a not uncommon occurrence in many circumstances, and a desire to identify the exact combination of factors or drivers in the Israeli-Palestinian instance. There was less urgency and passion, more detachment and reflection.

On the question: 'What are the origins of the conflict? *in the beginning*, the respondents recounted the horrors perpetrated against the Palestinians by Jews/Zionists/colonizers over the years up until and climaxing in the *Nakba* of 1948. For example, one wrote: 'The horrific ethnic cleansing which was planned and implemented by those who founded the state of Israel was, from a Zionist perspective, a way to solve the Jewish question. Needless to say, the immoral solution created another question, the Palestine question.' In discerning a plot, this response resembled those of some of the 'comparator group' of Palestinians discussed above.

Another of the Olive Tree Palestinians writing in 2013 defined the causes of the conflict as: 'Colonial aspirations and the occupation of Palestine in very militarized and vicious forms, displacing hundreds of thousands of people into the Diaspora.' Yet another, however, did distinguish between the conflict in the past and today, proposing that now the conflict is driven by Israel's ambitions to take all the land, forcing the (Palestinian) owners of that land to 'keep defending because if they do not they will be out of the game'.

At the end, the 5th cohort Palestinian responses still depicted a conqueror and a victim and still listed the types of crimes committed. However, they also showed some reflection on what these offences implied for the perpetrator, namely that divisions were emerging inside Israeli society and that Israelis are grappling with the consequences of their victories. The parallel depiction of the Palestinians was of 'unarmed and innocent civilians'. They made no mention of the role of the Arab states in 1948, unlike their Israeli counterparts, though in both sets of responses the Palestinians did show a sense of the wrongs done to Jews by the Europeans.

———

To conclude, in brief, the main themes to emerge from the survey with respect to the origins of the conflict, irrespective of exposure to dialogue, were: first, both Israelis and Palestinians identified the contemporary conflict as beginning with Jewish migration to what became Mandate Palestine in the late nineteenth and early twentieth century, though many also made reference to Biblical times as relevant to understanding the conflict. The site of the conflict was called Palestine by the Palestinians and Eretz Israel by the Jewish Israelis. Second, for most Israelis it was the hostility of the Arabs to the migrations that started the conflict and for most Palestinians it was the deeds and objectives of the Jewish Israelis that provoked it.

Third, most Israelis saw their national movement and aspirations as independent of and predating that of the Palestinians, while the latter defined their national resistance as a natural response to first Zionism and then Israeli actions, and more specifically the occupation. Yet, irrespective of whose national consciousness came first, as it were, both Israelis and Palestinians saw the conflict as a contest between two competing nationalist movements. Fourth, both groups described a conflict trajectory, with key milestones, among which 1948 featured prominently. Fifth, the Palestinians showed much more concern about post-1967 developments and the effect of the occupation on Palestinian daily lives than did the Israelis.

In their responses the Olive Tree alumni demonstrated a deeper knowledge and appreciation of the factors at the root of the conflict than did the non-Olive Tree respondents. Jewish Israeli alumni accorded more respect to the national aspirations of the Palestinians than the non-Olive Tree Jewish Israelis. Palestinian Olive Tree alumni were as exercised as their non-Olive Tree compatriots about the injustices experienced by the Palestinians, but were more tempered or sensitive in their use of terminology about the Israelis. Thus, among Israelis, cross-conflict dialogue can erode assumptions of superiority and build a greater sense of equality with 'the other', but as a consequence make them feel less secure. And for Palestinians dialogue can enhance self-confidence but does nothing to assuage their resentment of their relative deprivation.

5
Facts on the Ground

The facts on the ground keep changing in Israel and Palestine (Israel-Palestine, or Palestine/Israel). Over the past hundred years, many place names have changed, multiple villages have been levelled, and several new towns constructed. The de facto internal *and* external borders have shifted substantially. The population has expanded, and its ethnic/sectarian distribution has been reconfigured. Layers of new laws and regulations have been introduced and land ownership titles reassigned. Some areas have been designated 'state land', others 'nature reserves' and 'national forests', and yet others 'closed military zones.' Concrete barriers, fences and check points have been erected and others removed. New multi-lane highways and 'bypass roads' criss-cross the landscape, isolating some towns and connecting new ones. Various categories of colour-coded vehicle license plates have been invented. A confusing array of personal ID cards and permits have been introduced.

How you interpret all these changes rather depends on who you are. In each of the prevailing national narratives there is no denial of the 'facts on the ground', but they each assign different meanings to both the details and the big picture. Broadly speaking, in the Israeli national narrative the evolving physical and regulatory arrangements are depicted as necessary security measures, while in the Palestinian narrative they are defined as the infrastructure of occupation and dispossession. Yet neither one nor the other captures the entirety by itself, they are two sides of the same coin, experienced quite differently depending on whether you are Israeli or Palestinian.

The 'facts' and the 'narratives' are thus so intertwined that they have to be taken in conjunction to fully comprehend the situation. And the identities of the Palestinians and the Israelis are defined by their asymmetrical relations and circumstances, as well as their respective histories. They, like all of us, learn who they are not only as a result of what they are told but also through their experience and way of life, and how that compares to how others live.

For the most part Palestinians hate the way they are obliged to live, under occupation and without the rights that they see Israelis enjoy. By contrast, Israelis suffer none of the frustrations of the occupation and do not question the rights and freedoms that their statehood provides. They vary, however, in their levels of consciousness about Palestinian relative deprivation and their role in that. Some of those who are uncomfortable about the situation of the Palestinians find solace in the narrative that justifies the occupation on the basis of the dangers to their own security that it ascribes to Palestinian hatred of them.

In this context, I do not think it useful to attempt a detailed survey of 'the facts on the ground'. To do so would imply either giving a blow by blow account of who did what (and to whom) during the course of the conflict, or else focusing on the measures taken by successive Israeli governments to assert control over the Palestinian population and the results thereof. The former approach would take for ever and never be a complete list, while the latter would risk bringing a sense of order and one-sided purpose to an ever-evolving human drama. There are, in any case, plenty of both types of assessments of the situation available and I do not wish to replicate these.

Instead, I wish to emphasise the point that what you see and what meaning you attribute to that, depends on who you are and how you experience the 'facts on the ground'. Before recounting more survey findings, therefore, the following introduction to these is an essentially personal take on the situation, intertwined with some anecdotes from the Olive Tree. I have been visiting Palestine and Israel at least once a year for nearly three decades. Every time there is something new to take in. Overall, my impression is one of a constantly changing landscape, ever more scarring interventions on that landscape, and dogged determination, by the warring parties, to either control or resist the other.

The Evolving Landscape

When I made my first visit to Israel and Palestine in 1989, many of the Israelis and Palestinians subsequently selected for Olive Tree scholarships had not even been born and the rest were still children. At that time the first Palestinian 'Intifada' or uprising (in Arabic the term means literally 'shaking off') was in full flow and clashes between stone-throwing demonstrators and armed troops were a regular occurrence across the West Bank and Gaza Strip. Nonetheless, I was able to travel around and explore all over Israel and the Occupied Territories. In the latter, initially I availed myself of a guide from the local offices of UNRWA, the agency that ran the Palestinian refugee camps and, along with other bodies, recorded all the clashes and monitored the evolving 'facts on the ground'.

Inside Israel I used public transport to make my way around. I took an official guided tour of the Golan Heights. I explored Haifa, much of Tel Aviv, Jaffa and Jerusalem on foot. I visited Yad Vashem. I was given a guided tour of some of the Israeli monuments to the battles fought in 1948 and 1967. Since my intention on that first visit, which lasted three months, was to study British-Israeli relations, I interviewed many Israelis – businessmen, canteen staff, writers, journalists, academics, politicians, former military – and they were all very welcoming and forthcoming. Between them they gave me a thorough introduction to the broadly secular Ashkenazi narrative on the founding of the state and its trajectory thereafter.

Once I started making weekend visits to Jerusalem, staying in a convent guest house in the Muslim quarter of the Old City, I came face to face frequently with the almost daily skirmishes that characterised the Intifada at the time. I began talking to young Palestinians, starting with some of the staff at the guest house, and thus began my explorations into the Palestinian story. In addition, since my hostel hosted Christian clerics and scholars on pilgrimage to the various holy sites, I benefitted from their extensive knowledge of Biblical history. It was in such company that I first visited the Western Wall, Masada, Jericho and Bethlehem.

At one point, I rented a car, having learned sufficient Hebrew to read the road signs, not all of which provided an English transliteration of the place names. In the West Bank and Gaza most signs gave the names only in Arabic at that time, or in Arabic and Hebrew. It was not my intention, however, to drive the rented car into the Occupied Territories. That said, I had little way of knowing where the dividing line was at the time, between the Occupied Territories and 'Israel proper' (as it became known), because that line was not marked on any of the tourist maps I was able to buy.[1] An Israeli friend had to help me out by putting a mark on each of the main roads running East-West that linked Israel to the territories it captured from Jordan in 1967. The old border or armistice line ('the Green Line') between Israel and the West Bank was dismantled by the Israelis in 1967, including inside Jerusalem (the Eastern side of which Israel subsequently annexed).

As I learned in 1989, even though the physical border around the West

---

[1] In December 1967 the Israeli government decided to erase the 1949 Armistice Line (the Green Line) from all the maps, atlases and textbooks it published. See Weizman, E. (2007) *Hollow Land: Israel's Architecture of Occupation* London & New York: Verso, p. 18.

Bank had been removed, the movement of Palestinians from there into Israel was subject to control through a permit system.[2] Many hundreds of them were recruited for labouring and service jobs inside 'Israel proper', but unless their individual permits allowed for it, they were not permitted to stay overnight. The Gaza Strip, unlike the West Bank, was surrounded by a perimeter fence, but access and exit through the main Erez crossing point was possible with the right permit and, in my case, with a British passport. That said, when the Israeli authorities deemed fit, they would institute a 'closure' which meant access to Israel was denied to Palestinians until the closure was lifted. Impromptu military checkpoints on the main roads were the method used to control movement.

During my initial visits to the Gaza Strip there were Israeli soldiers to be seen everywhere and the possibility of violence breaking out was ever present. I was struck by how small the Gaza Strip was, how crowded and how poor, even then. Donkey carts, battered, fume-belching cars and ill-shod or barefoot children milled around in the streets, many of which were not paved. Things would improve for a while following the Oslo Accords, when foreign investment enabled a general clean-up of the main streets. Restaurants appeared along the beachfront and some of the barbed wire removed from the beaches themselves. In 2005 the Israeli settlers and troops evacuated, though without coordination with the PA, and following the Hamas takeover in Gaza in 2007, the Strip came under an Israeli administered blockade, which international donors protested, but failed to remove. My own visits to Gaza ended at that point. By all accounts conditions there have progressively worsened since.

I did however continue visiting Israel and the West Bank, both for my own research and, in the 1990s and early 2000s, to undertake joint projects with both Palestinians and Israelis, mostly separately, and in one case with Jordanian and Palestinian colleagues, when we criss-crossed the Jordan to spend time on both sides.[3] I was therefore able to see how the border crossing operated at the

---

[2] I published two works summarising the findings of that first trip: Hollis, R. (1989) 'Tactical Dynamics of the *Intifada* and Israel's Response' *RUSI Journal* 134(4); and Hollis, R. (1990) 'Israel on the Brink of Decision: Division, Unity and Crosscurrents in the Israeli Body Politic' RISCT *Conflict Studies*, No. 231.

[3] We published the findings of that project, which was funded by the Ford Foundation, in Hamarneh, M., Rosemary Hollis and Khalil Shikaki (1997) *Jordanian-Palestinian Relations: Where To?* London: The Royal Institute of International Affairs, also published in Arabic in Amman and separately in Nablus.

Allenby Bridge, between Jordan and the West Bank. That has remained the main, and now *only*, route out of the West Bank permitted to the Palestinians by the Israelis and the Jordanians. To this day, the Jordanians do not treat Allenby (now called the King Hussein bridge) as an official international border and internationals such as myself have to have a visa from the Jordanian authorities in advance, to use it to enter Jordan. Following the peace treaty between Israel and Jordan of 1994 an official crossing was opened north of the West Bank (the Sheikh Hussein Bridge), for use by Israeli citizens, most often Palestinians with Israeli passports, and internationals.

I relate all of this because the details are illustrative of the complicated procedures that have evolved over time to control the movement of Palestinians between their homes and the rest of the world. During the time I was director of the Olive Tree Programme (2008-16), the procedures became progressively more onerous. All West Bank Palestinians could expect to have their luggage searched at the Allenby bridge and had to be cleared by the Jordanian government to transit to Jordan's main airport and thence fly to London. East Jerusalem Palestinians, who hold a travel document or 'laissez-passer' issued by the Israelis, though not Israeli citizenship, may use Israel's Ben Gurion airport. Some of them also have Jordanian passports, but these do not entitle them to live in Jordan.

Gazan Palestinians used to be able to enter Egypt at the Rafah crossing point and proceed from there, via Cairo, to London. However, the queues at Rafah were usually so extensive that they could not count on completing the crossing on any one day and had to use 'connections' (*wasta*) to jump the queue. One told me he was offered assisted passage by an Israeli soldier at the border, on condition he agreed to 'cooperate'. He declined, but then had to wait for longer. If the melee on the Palestinian side was particularly chaotic, Palestinian border police could fire in the air, to restore order, which made the crossing dangerous. Once over, they only had transit rights and could expect to be held in detention overnight at Cairo airport to prevent them exiting the airport before their flight.

The journey back to Gaza was even more unpredictable and risky. The Egyptian authorities could suddenly decide to close the border and keep it closed for days or weeks and they would thereby face the possibility of not making it home or being stuck there if they did. Consequently, almost all the Gazan Palestinians who participated in the Olive Tree decided not to risk going home for visits for the duration of their three-year degree courses. By 2015 relations between Egypt and the Hamas leadership, which seized internal control of Gaza in 2007, were so bad that the Egyptians closed the border almost entirely. Then the only way out was to have Israeli permission to exit via Erez, be escorted across Israel and on to Jericho, then leave via Allenby – provided, that is, the Jordanians permitted them transit to the airport. The exact timing of their exit from Erez had to be coordinated with both the Israelis and the Jordanians in advance.

In 2008 a member of staff at the British Consulate-General in Jerusalem could be asked to help with these procedures and be the escort across Israel. However, by 2011 the British government had outsourced visa processing for Palestinians to the UK Border Agency offices in Amman and there was no longer a staff member in Jerusalem to help. Initially there was a person I could speak to at the UK Border Agency in Amman to solicit help, at least in processing a Palestinian visa application. In due course this also became impossible and we learned that the agency staff were instructed to find reasons to deny a visa if possible. Meanwhile, the UK Government delegated to the UK universities responsibility for ensuring all international student visa applications were in order, on penalty of losing their licence to admit international students if they were negligent and/or made mistakes. That fate befell London Metropolitan University, though thankfully not City.

The newly arduous procedure for processing student visa applications also affected the Israelis awarded Olive Tree scholarships in the latter years of the programme, though never to the same extent as the Palestinians. For a while, Israeli applications were processed at an office in Turkey, having been submitted in Tel Aviv initially. In a couple of instances small mistakes on their forms meant that they had to reapply and risk being late for the start of the academic year.

Meanwhile, from the time of the second Palestinian Intifada in 2000, freedom of movement inside the West Bank became more difficult for all Palestinians. Work permits to enter Israel ceased to be issued and access to East Jerusalem, even to file a visa application, was routinely denied. The reasons for the new strictures were of course the security concerns that affected all Israelis in the face of the suicide bomb attacks and knife assaults perpetrated by Palestinians inside Israeli cities and towns, on buses, in bars and restaurants, and, on one occasion, at a Passover *Seder* and on another, inside a synagogue. As one Olive Tree Israeli participant growing up in Jerusalem later recounted, it was a terrifying time, wondering every day whether he would be injured or killed in one of the attacks.

I personally continued my frequent visits during this period. I found my Israeli friends were reluctant to dine out in restaurants, where bag searches were routine and the atmosphere was always tense. Anyone looking even vaguely Arab was an object of suspicion. My friends who had teenage children were constantly worried and checking their phones for fear that they had come to harm. One Israeli, a former peace activist, told me how 'let down' he felt, including by Palestinians he had previously regarded as friends, working for a common cause. He said the only way he could cope was to preoccupy himself watching movies and by making regular trips abroad, to escape the tension. Like so many other things I have heard over the years, I absorbed this information as exactly that, information – not an invitation to cast judgement.

When I went to the West Bank during the second Intifada it was difficult to get around and the situation at check points was fractious and volatile. The main road from Jerusalem to Ramallah was bulldozed and the Qalandia checkpoint reconfigured, with the installation of a new so-called 'terminal', with turnstiles and bag checks which everyone had to transit on foot. On a couple of occasions when the terminal was under construction I remember being completely disorientated and anxious as I tried to find my way through the disorganised lines of soldiers, disgruntled Palestinians, heaps of rubble and ploughed up areas.

Once the new 'terminal' was in operation to enter Ramallah I would have to take a bus to Qalandia then leave the bus to walk through the terminal, have my passport and bags checked, then find new transport on the other side. Getting from there to Nablus was hazardous and difficult during the second Intifada. Once things calmed down, and the PA started to function again, I took a bus from Ramallah to Nablus to visit one of the Olive Tree students and his family. He took me round the old city or 'kasbah' as some called it. On past visits I had been struck by how like the one in Damascus the old city was: narrow winding alleyways, old buildings, multiple spice shops, business and bustle. This historic heart of Nablus, once a commercial hub, was badly damaged when the Israeli forces reoccupied the area in 2002 and on my visit in 2009 I was saddened to see how fragile and precarious the reconstruction effort had left the buildings, and how comparatively subdued were the streets.

The Israeli response to the terrorism of the second Intifada, instigated by Ariel Sharon when he became Prime Minister in early 2001, was to send Israeli

forces back into the West Bank Palestinian population centres previously evacuated under the Oslo Accords. They disarmed and dismantled the Palestinian
police, fought running battles with protestors, using tear-gas, rubber bullets and
on occasion live fire, arrested hundreds, and instituted curfews.

The Palestinians, according to Sharon, had to learn to 'lower their expectations'. The Israeli forces also ransacked PA offices, captured and confiscated
PA records (including computer hard disks) and laid siege to Yasser Arafat in
his Ramallah headquarters – from which he was never to emerge until he suc-
cumbed to illness and was airlifted to hospital in France, where he subsequently
died from as yet unverified causes.

For Olive Tree Palestinians growing up in Gaza and the West Bank in the
early years of this century their experiences during the second Intifada were
formative. Later, under the auspices of the Olive Tree Programme, they listened
to the stories of their Israeli counterparts about how terrifying life was in Israel
at that time. Yet, they could not concede that this justified the collective punishment which, as far as they were concerned, they had been subjected to. One
of them, whose home was occupied by Israeli soldiers and his bedroom used by
an Israeli sniper, while he, his mother and one of his siblings were forced out
into the street even though a curfew had been instigated, the memories were
still vivid.

It was during the second Intifada that Sharon decided to build the barrier
that now cordons off most of the West Bank from Israel. It follows the Green
Line in some places and in others cuts into the West Bank. It circles the eastern
outskirts of Jerusalem, dissecting Palestinian neighbourhoods. Elsewhere it has
isolated some communities from the orchards and crops on which their liveli-
hoods have depended. Farmers have to await the arrival of soldiers to open the
gates leading to their fields and these may not be reopened until the harvested
produce has wilted in the sun. If farmers fail to tend their crops for three con-
secutive years, their land may be confiscated under Israeli law. In some places
Palestinians could only access their orchards via deep sheer-sided gulleys, cut
into the terrain below road level and intersected by heavy metal gates. Going
through one of these, I was unnerved to think what it would be like to be
trapped there, in the event that the gates were closed.

Everywhere in the West Bank these days, the landscape has been trans-
formed by the construction of Jewish settlements, mostly built on hilltops, looking down upon Palestinian towns and villages. Some settlements are built on

confiscated land, others on so-called 'state land'. While they have proliferated since 1967, sometimes under Labour-led Israeli governments, sometimes under those of Likud, Palestinians are not permitted to build in most parts of the West Bank, even on land they own. According to the Israeli Peace Now movement's Settlement Watch,[4] the number of Jewish settlements in the West Bank, excluding East Jerusalem, officially established by the Israeli government, totalled 132 in 2017. A further 106 so-called 'outposts', illegal under Israeli law, had also been established. The total number of Jewish settlers had reached 413,400 by 2017. The number of Israeli settlements in East Jerusalem was thirteen and the number of Israelis living in East Jerusalem had reached 214,710, giving the Jews an overall majority of 63 percent within the municipal boundaries redrawn by Israel after 1967.[5]

Those settlement blocks closest to 'Israel proper' now lie on the western side of the security barrier. Others are linked to Israel by roads and highways that Palestinians are not permitted to use. According to the UN Office for Coordination of Humanitarian Affairs (OCHA), which keeps detailed records: 'Over 400 kilometres of roads are prohibited or highly restricted for Palestinian-plated vehicles, excluding military roads and roads inside settlements', forcing an estimated 88,000 Palestinians to make long detours to reach the nearest town or service centre.[6] By the end of 2016 there were 572 fixed roadblocks or obstacles to movement inside the West Bank, some permanently staffed, others as deemed necessary to control movement.[7]

In the aftermath of the second Intifada, through international intervention, the PA was reconstituted, including the Palestinian police force, for which the United States, Canada and the EU provided training and equipment. They operate only within certain areas, in accordance with arrangements originally agreed in the Oslo Accords in the 1990s.

One of the facets of the occupation which has most bemused me over the years has been the complex political geography devised during the 1990s as part of the Oslo process and which was supposed to be an interim arrangement, but

---

[4] See http://peacenow.org.il/en/settlements-watch/settlements-data/population

[5] http://peacenow.org.il/en/settlements-watch/settlements-data/jerusalem

[6] https://www.ochaopt.org/content/west-bank-movement-and-access-west-bank

[7] https://www.ochaopt.org/content/west-bank-movement-and-access-west-bank

which has endured. Under Oslo, the West Bank was divided into areas A, B and C, with A being the main Palestinian population centres, B the surrounding villages (together constituting about 28 percent of the whole West Bank) and C the remainder. Area A is now under PA control in all aspects of civil administration and internal (police) security. In Area B the PA has charge of civil administration but shares security control with the Israelis.

Israelis surveyed for this book frequently referred to the West Bank as if it were mostly under the remit of the PA, though it is not. In Area C (approximately 60 percent of the West Bank) the Israelis have retained full control and Israeli forces still enter Palestinian cities and villages in Areas A and B at will, sometimes in night raids, to make arrests.

These are the circumstances that underlie the responses of West Bank Palestinians to my survey questions who saw 'Oslo' as the starting point of the conflict, as reported in the previous chapter. The foregoing summary of the constantly changing 'facts on the ground' also suggests what was in the minds of all the Palestinians surveyed, Olive Tree alumni and others, when they answered my questions about what they want now, as detailed below. All the Olive Tree Palestinians had tales to tell about their experiences at Israeli checkpoints. One told how he was trying to drive his pregnant sister, already in labour, to the nearest hospital, and was held up at a checkpoint while the soldiers satisfied themselves that he and his sister were not 'a threat'. Others also had tales of being taken or called in for questioning.

For some years now, Palestinian men and boys between the ages of sixteen and thirty can expect to be taken in by the Israeli forces periodically, sometimes just for questioning, other times for indefinite detention. The possibility of such episodes keeps them in a constant state of nervousness. I discovered the implications of this when I was selecting candidates for the Olive Tree, between 2008 and 2013. It was my normal procedure, during the interviews, to ask the candidates how they thought they would handle a confrontation with an Israeli counterpart, for example in the residence halls and after some alcohol had been consumed. 'How might you react' I asked, 'if you find yourself rowing with an Israeli who had served in the IDF and who threatens you?' On a few such occasions I was saddened to witness the candidates literally crumple before my eyes and lose all the self-confidence they had previously displayed.

As it turned out, and presumably in part because all the Olive Tree participants were on their guard and had been cautioned to take care, if such rows did occur, they did not come to physical blows. Even so, in the formal dialogue sessions there were heated arguments and tempers could flare, especially when participants recounted their personal experiences or touched on sensitive issues like the Palestinian terrorist attacks that had endangered and frightened all Israeli civilians, or Palestinian experiences of IDF actions, house searches and summary detention. And as this illustrates, even though the Olive Tree experience took place in London, in a university setting, miles away from the battle zone, the conflict was ever present in the dialogue.

When the conflict flared into hot war, as it did on the Gaza front in 2008-09, 2012 and 2014, it proved impossible for the Olive Tree participants to detach themselves sufficiently to continue dialogue with 'the enemy' in London. At these times, my colleagues and I, as the facilitators, concentrated on supporting and helping all the individuals in the programme to cope with their distress and anxiety. Those who came from Gaza and had families at risk experienced the most pain. But all the participants questioned the purpose and morality of meeting 'the other' at such times. For their part, many Israelis could barely communicate their fraught and divided emotions and in one instance two of them resorted to doing so through art not speech, and another through music.

At these times I personally felt the presence of a threatening force of destruction that could wipe away overnight all the hard work that had been put into better understanding. My instincts, with which my colleagues concurred, during the 2014 war, led us to decide to meet the Olive Tree participants in separate national groups for a while – the better to enable them to tend to their needs and build some new solidarity with their own, before again encountering the other. I learned something that the School for Peace approach, discussed in Chapter 1, has long advocated – namely that nurturing national group self-awareness and confidence is *as* essential to cross-conflict dialogue as mediated encounters with the other.

During the period when the Palestinians and Israelis in Olive Tree met in separate groups, in late 2014 and early 2015, it was my colleague Damian who designed and led a series of activities to enable the two groups to regain some calm and confidence. He devised some scenes or sketches for the groups to 'act out' or 'role play' – among which he included various family occasions or crises and even, for example, altercations at checkpoints. The effect was to take them out of their immediate preoccupations, use their imagination, be creative, laugh even and relieve some of their stress. They 'rebuilt some ground', as Damian might put it, and went on to write their own sketches. Performing some of these to the other group then enabled a reconnection between them.

I mention this partly because I was so inspired by and appreciative of Damian's insight into what the situation required, and partly because it illustrates very well how experiences inform us *and* stay with us. Most of all, the activity demonstrated how well we know the scripts assigned to us *and*, that it is possible to discover how to write our own.

With the foregoing summary as background, I would like to turn now to the responses of the Israelis and Palestinians I surveyed in 2016, to two questions. These were: 'What do the Palestinians want now?' and 'What do the Israelis want now?' Their answers were the most revealing of the entire survey. In contrast to those Israelis who had not been exposed to dialogue with 'the other', the Israeli Olive Tree alumni who had, proved far more aware of what the Palestinians themselves assert they want. Among the Palestinian respondents, however, there was not much difference between the answers of the Olive Tree alumni and those of the non-Olive Tree 'comparator group' to either question.

The message here is that for the Palestinians there is no escape from, or forgiveness of, the pervasive consequences of the occupation. For most Israelis, by contrast, the occupation can be ignored or denied, because it does not directly affect their freedom of movement or human rights, and, given their lack of contact with ordinary Palestinians, their theories about what motivates the latter are essentially just that – theories – based on their collective fears or narratives, rather than knowledge.

Again, I refer the reader to Chapter 2, pages 48-51 for the details of how the survey was conducted and the attendant caveats.

Israeli Views on 'What the Palestinians Want Now'

When posed the question: 'What do the Palestinians want now?' most of the non-Olive Tree Israeli respondents identified a range of positions on the Palestinian side. One said:

It depends on who you ask. The fundamentalists want all of Palestine, while the moderates will be satisfied with the 1967 borders. However, the average person on the street will ask only for quiet [*as in 'peace and quiet'*] and stability for his family.

Another said it was difficult to generalise, and the spotlight is mostly on 'the extreme Palestinian groups.' Of these, he/she said:

In their fantasies, a large percentage of the Palestinians would like to see Israel disappear (perhaps because of propaganda within Palestinian society, and perhaps not – this requires further research), but I believe there are also Palestinians who view Israel as a positive element in the region – not just economically – and would therefore like to continue living alongside Israel or in Israel.

Yet another respondent from the non-Olive Tree 'comparator group' identified a spectrum of views among Palestinians: from those who would settle for sovereignty in 'agreed upon territories'; to 'a segment' that 'insists' on exercising "the Right of Return"[8] for all Palestinians (and their descendants) who lived in the land before 1948'; to some extremists who wish to take over all of 'Palestine' and expel the Jews; to yet others who want 'to exterminate the Jews altogether'.

The general message in the non-Olive Tree responses was that Palestinian 'realists' would settle for a two-state solution, but only one respondent thought such pragmatists represented a majority. More prominent was the perception that the Palestinians generally still harbour unrealistic demands and are hostile to Jews and/or Jewish predominance. One respondent also thought that facts on the ground were rendering a Palestinian state unrealistic and therefore Palestinians were increasingly inclined to consider one binational state as the next best thing. Not a single one of the non-Olive Tree respondents mentioned 'end of occupation' as such.

---

[8] The term 'Right of Return' has become a sort of Palestinian dictum or prayer, based on UN Resolution 194 of December 1948 – which resolved that 'refugees wishing to return to their homes and live at peace with their neighbours should be permitted to do so at the earliest practicable date' – but which also sits in juxtaposition to the Israeli 'Law of Return' of 1950 which gives Jews the 'right of return' and the right to live in Israel. Throughout all peace negotiations the Israelis have maintained that were the Palestinian refugees of 1948 and their descendants permitted to exercise the Right of Return in accordance with UN Resolution 194, Palestinians could thereby vastly outnumber the Jewish population of Israel. Palestinians maintain that their 'right' must be recognised, even if they choose or are persuaded/compensated not to do so. The issue has remained one of the sticking points in all official negotiations to date.

In stark contrast, aside from one who discerned ambivalence on the Palestinian side, all the Israeli Olive Tree alumni acknowledged or recognised that the Palestinians want an end to their present conditions in the West Bank and Gaza Strip. They used terms like: 'end to occupation', 'freedom', 'independence', 'a state' and 'normal lives'. In addition, several said the Palestinians want both a state and the 'Right of Return', which, in Israeli discourse generally constitutes supplanting the Jewish majority in Israel or a binational state. Two examples illustrate the general picture:

> I am not sure that it is correct to phrase the question in this manner. It is obvious that different audiences have different desires and perspectives. Within the [*Palestinian*] 'basket of wants' there is a desire for self-determination through the establishment of a state, for sane lives in which their rights are guaranteed, for some sort of an improvement in their daily lives and for 'ending' the Zionist state and returning to what could have been.

And:

> The Palestinians want a state and freedom. The Palestinians want to be equal to, and have the same rights as, other people [*nations*] in the world. The Palestinians want to bring an end to the occupation and to the destructive wars in Gaza.

The Israelis who had participated in Olive Tree thus displayed a clear appreciation of what the Palestinians themselves say they want now – as demonstrated in the Palestinian responses to the same question, detailed below. Not only were the comparator group respondents less well informed in this regard, but also, they showed no awareness of the prevalence and specificity of the Palestinian desire/demand for 'an end to occupation'. In addition, the non-Olive Tree respondents asserted a level of support for a two-state solution among Palestinians which was not echoed among the Olive Tree Israeli alumni. Instead, the latter reported simply that the Palestinians find the status quo intolerable and want it to end – however that might be achieved. The alumni did not, however, venture an opinion on whether Palestinian demands can or should be met.

Israeli Views on 'What the Israelis Want Now'

All the Israeli responses to the question: 'What do the Israelis want now?' identified a diversity of opinion among Israelis, considerable resistance to compromise, and/or ambivalence. In contrast to the way in which some of the non-Olive Tree Israeli respondents had discerned the existence of 'realists' or pragmatists among the Palestinians who would 'settle for' a state in the West Bank, they did not identify a commensurate group of Israeli 'realists' ready to meet the Palestinians half way, as it were. Instead, they indicated a readiness among some Israelis to agree to a separate Palestinian state, within limits, in the interests of protecting the Jewish majority in Israel, and even these, they believed, would not compromise much on Jerusalem or accept the exercise of the 'Right of Return' by Palestinians. One non-Olive Tree respondent described the problem thus:

As for the Israelis, the inability to determine what they want is the heart of the problem. The divisions regarding the conflict best reflect the fact that, today, the state of Israel does not have one unifying goal or an agreed upon objective. And the differences of opinions regarding this issue touch upon the core of the Zionist vision and the way in which it is realised. If we do try to make some rough generalisations, there are two main streams of thought within the Israeli discourse: the first is interested in separating from the Palestinians. It is entrapped in the 'Oslo Paradigm' which stipulates two states, and the principle guiding it is maintaining a Jewish liberal state. It is therefore viable, in their view, to establish borders, place a fence and separate from the Palestinians soon. The second stream opposes the concession of any parts of the land in order to reach a political settlement and it proposes a continuation of the existing situation, following the rationale that the reality on the ground will win. Meaning, the continuation of the settlements in Judea and Samaria[9] and an Israeli presence there will lead to an irreversible situation which will eventually make the Palestinians realise that there is no hope for change. Many within this stream integrate religious foundations into their beliefs, which makes fertile ground for believing that 'what should happen will happen' and that eventually the

---

[9] 'Judea and Samaria' is the official Israeli designation for 'the West Bank' of the river Jordan, ruled by Jordan between 1948 and 1967, then captured and occupied by Israel.

Zionist ethos will overcome the Palestinian one.

Another non-Olive Tree respondent said:

> The Second Intifada led many in the Israeli public to lose faith in the ability to reach a peace agreement with the Palestinians. The Israeli reaction to terrorism, in the form of operation Defensive Shield,[10] was harsh and weakened the Palestinian leadership. But it also led to the fact that, over the past decade, no cycle of violence reached a similar extent. The withdrawal of Israel from Gaza in 2005 and Hamas's takeover of this territory led many Israelis to believe that it is impossible to return territories to the Palestinians in a way which will not critically jeopardise Israel's security. Today, the Israeli public is divided in its stance regarding the future of the Israeli-Palestinian conflict. While the idea of dividing the land and establishing a Palestinian state alongside Israel still grabs a hold amongst nearly half of the Israeli public, it seems that, in practice, the majority of Israelis prefer the continuation of the current situation (the 'status quo') and they are willing to pay the price of the conflict (terrorist waves, repeated operations in Gaza, a few dozen dead Israelis a year). The government of Israel expresses a total lack of confidence in the Palestinian side and it acts to deepen the Jewish settlement in the West Bank in order to establish 'facts on the ground' and prevent the possibility of returning these territories as part of a future agreement.

The Israeli Olive Tree alumni were generally more succinct in their responses. For example, one said that 'the Israelis want peace and security' and another that: 'The Israelis want quiet (i.e. peace and quiet) and security. They want to be given the opportunity to live their lives, while realising their aspirations in the occupied territories.' Yet another said: 'on the one hand' the Israelis want 'security' and 'on the other hand, a maintenance of the existing status quo when it comes to the occupation of the territories, the separation policy, building in the settlements and so on.'

In the relative brevity of the alumni responses I sense a kind of impatience

---

[10] Operation Defensive Shield was the military operation launched against what was termed the Palestinian 'infrastructure of terror' following the deadly bomb attack on a Jewish Passover seder in Natanya in March 2002.

with the question, an assertion that 'it should be obvious' what they want, from their behaviour. At the same time, however, they were not particularly critical. Their list of Israeli wants included: 'peace and security' and pursuit of their goals in the West Bank; an end to Palestinian violence; an end to 'the boycott'; 'international acceptance' and 'respect'. In one encapsulation the Israelis were deemed to want 'no land for peace'.

Broadly, however, the prevailing view among the Israeli Olive Tree alumni was that compromise is not on the cards. More poignantly, one respondent reflected that: 'many people do not acknowledge the occupation or the very existence of the Palestinian people (nation)' and another intimated that the Israelis want 'the other' to change not them.

Overall, my sense is that, compared to the comparator group respondents, the alumni were more aware of the distance between the Israeli and Palestinian narratives and saw Israelis in general as identifying 'the other,' rather than 'the occupation,' as the problem.

Palestinian Views on 'What the Palestinians Want Now'

All the Palestinian responses to this question highlighted their desire to feel safe and enjoy security, as well as have freedom of movement both within and beyond the occupied territories, without fear. According to one non-Olive Tree respondent:

> We want to feel we are living in our country. This is our country. They make us feel like we are the Zionists who don't have any right to this land. We want freedom of movement, safety and security. We are rejected in our own country and outside it.

Another said: 'we live in fear and terror because of the occupation'.

In respect of their daily life one respondent (non-Olive Tree) called for the revocation of the Paris Protocol (by which the Israeli and Palestinian economies are integrated – with the same prices and taxes in operation). He/she called for this, on the grounds that it 'is killing us slowly'. The full response ran as follows:

> First of all, we would like to be safe. Second of all, we want to revoke this horrible agreement called the Paris Protocol. It is killing us slowly. This

Protocol attached our economy to the Israeli economy. Our average income is maybe 10% of the average income in Israel and yet the prices are almost the same. This is a very important thing to do. We want to be able to move easily like the rest of the people. We want to be able to take our passport and then go wherever we want. We are not allowed to go anywhere. I'm banned from travelling.

Another called for 'internal and external justice' and another said:

I want to feel that the passport I carry is a real passport that allows me to travel to any country I wish, not just to Jordan. I feel I'm living in a big prison called Palestine. The economy is very important – our average income is a small fraction of theirs and the costs are the same. I don't want to be ruled by two governments like I am now. Palestinian police and Israeli police can fine us alike. We pay customs to both sides. I feel like I live in one country, but one ruled by two governments.

Others called for refugee return and to go back to live 'where my ancestors lived but not with an Israeli ID'. And there was a plea for 'dignity' and 'the same rights as anybody else'.

Turning to the Palestinian Olive Tree alumni, one's response would seem to endorse the Israeli suppositions about Palestinian 'realists.' She said:

I will be realistic, and I won't say expelling the Jews from Palestine and restoring the stolen land. I know many generations have been born on this land and don't know anything except Israel as a country. Personally, I want a one state solution with equal rights for everyone under a democratic system. But I'm also realistic and know that this will never happen. And since I'm the weaker side in this conflict and don't have the strength to negotiate this solution I accept the two states solution on the 1967 borders even though this would break my heart. I'm a Palestinian who lived most of her life in Gaza. As a pessimistic person I know that even this won't happen. To be honest this question really annoys me. What do the Palestinians want? It's like we have the power or the ability to make anything happen. This is a rhetorical question and answering it won't change anything.

Similarly, another alumnus said:

> There is a difference between what the Palestinians want and what they
> are willing to settle for. It also depends which Palestinians. Their expec-
> tations lower with time. The greater that their suffering becomes the less
> they want. For example, the (Gaza) Palestinians might settle for an end to
> the siege and the Palestinians in the West Bank would probably settle for
> the occupation ending (or maybe even just the wall coming down, and an
> end to house demolitions, checkpoints, arrest and detention without charge
> etc). However, the Palestinians in Jordan, Syria etc would probably want
> different things. I want all the violence to end, equal rights, opportunities
> and justice for everyone regardless of their ethnicity, with free movement.

Other alumni were very succinct, coming up with answers including: 'Peace
and independence' and 'end of the occupation and the return of the refugees'.
These 'wants' capture the essence of all the responses. Even so, comparing the
Olive Tree alumni with the non-Olive Tree respondents, the former were more
emphatic in calling for an end to occupation, for freedom and for rights. The
non-Olive Tree respondents placed as much emphasis on personal safety as on
freedom.

Summing up the whole picture, one Olive Tree alumnus said: 'In the end
all Palestinians want to live a life free of violence, war, internal and international
political turmoil.' And another: 'They want to return to their lands, to live in stability and security and to carry on with their lives.' The same person also noted
that the Israelis want stability and security too.

Across the board the message from all the Palestinian respondents could
not be clearer – they want an end to occupation, 'normal lives', safety and freedom. This is more or less the same as what the Israelis said they want for themselves, but not the same as what the non-Olive Tree Israelis *think* the Palestinians want, as detailed previously.

Palestinian Views on 'What the Israelis Want Now'

The Palestinian responses to this question ranged across a spectrum. At one end
were claims that the Israelis want 'everything' or 'from the Nile to the Euphrates'
or 'to control the World'. At the other end, were statements like the following:

As a government they want to exist on the ground. They don't want more than that. They want to be supported from the outside. The people want to be happy.

And:

For now they want to co-exist. The Jews are like us, they want peace and a solution.

In between these extremes, one non-Olive Tree respondent said the Israelis want influence but not expansion. A more calibrated perspective was that:

They don't want peace. Maybe the ones who want peace are the leftists, but the right doesn't want peace.

And:

No one knows what the Jews want. Most of the prophets were sent for the Jews.

Another respondent reflected that there is 'what they claim they want' and what they show by their actions.

Overall, I detected little indication that the respondents believed there was a deal waiting to be done with the Israelis in the prevailing circumstances. Negative views of 'the other' and their ambitions were more prominent than potentially conciliatory views.

The responses of the Palestinian Olive Tree alumni were, if anything, more negative and strident than those of the non-Olive Tree respondents. One might deduce from this that there are consequences to building more group solidarity and self-confidence, as a facet of cross-conflict dialogue. Yet, if so, that is not necessarily a negative outcome for dialogue, since if agreement or peace were to mean simply the capitulation of the weaker party, that would not augur well for the durability of the agreement over time.

Most of the alumni depicted the Israelis as wanting to keep what they have, take more, be accepted as 'legitimate' and no longer be seen as the 'bad guys'. The Israelis were characterised as wanting to continue the occupation, but wanting the killing to stop while not allowing the Palestinians 'justice'. The Palestinian alumni displayed a belief that the Israelis are 'ignorant' of the price the Palestinians are paying for their (Israeli) freedom.

Essentially the Israelis were described by the Olive Tree alumni as *wanting* the very things that the Palestinians want an end to. As one put it: 'They want to live in stability and security', while the Palestinians want 'to return to their lands, to live in stability and security and to carry on with their lives'. As another alumnus phrased it:

> The Israelis want to live in what they call Israel in peace, without thinking about the reality of the Palestinian side – as if the conflict was coming from one side. As a result of the position of strength that Israel enjoys, I don't see how the Israeli individual or society can change their vision of the current Palestinian situation.

Taking stock overall, the Israeli Olive Tree alumni were able to identify what the Palestinians want in a way that showed more knowledge and aware-ness than non-Olive Tree Israeli respondents. However, the Olive Tree Pales-tinians voiced a perspective on the Israelis which was much more in keeping with that of the non-Olive Tree Palestinians.

In asserting that the Israelis *in general* either *actively want* those things which the Palestinians wish they could get rid of, or else *refuse to see* what the Palestinians have to put up with, as a price for Israeli freedoms – the Olive Tree Palestinian alumni showed no inclination to distinguish between what they thought about Israelis in general and what they knew about those they had met in person.

During the various Track II exercises[11] that took place during the 1990s, when the Oslo process was still in play, it was not uncommon for Palestinian and Israeli participants to say they could readily envisage making peace with their counterparts in such exercises, but their problem was with the rest of the two populations who were depicted as more belligerent and uncompromising. However, with the Olive Tree participants there was no indication of similar thinking and certainly not in their survey responses. This may well constitute a specific finding here, namely that the 'feel good' factor that often predominated

---

[11] Discussed in Chapter 1.

in semi-official dialogues cannot be replicated in such exercises at the people-to-people level, once their political leaders have abandoned peace-making.

How Views Evolved among Dialogue Participants

Israeli Participants

When asked 'What do the Palestinians want now?' in November 2013, the Israeli members of the fifth Olive Tree cohort indicated they already had an awareness of the desire of Palestinians to be rid of the occupation. Their responses to this question certainly contrasted with responses from the sample of non-Olive Tree Israeli respondents surveyed in 2016. This could suggest that in the space of just two months of intensive interaction across the divide, the message had got through that it was the lack of freedom and the insecurity felt by Palestinians that most concerned them.

By July 2016, this awareness was still evident, however it was mixed with an additional awareness of some of the ambiguities in the range of positions on both sides. By way of illustration, it is worth quoting one response in full:

> The obvious answer is establishing a state. However, the Palestinian leadership is not taking any of the steps required in order to establish a state and there is a sense that the Palestinians got used to their status as an occupied people, and that, in an illogical way, they even enjoy it. The Palestinian people are divided, and the leadership is dysfunctional. The situation on the ground is intolerable for the Palestinians and this leads to uprisings and resistance. It is unclear whether the goal is the establishment of an independent state or a relief in the conditions imposed by Israel. The quiet and the status quo blur the real desire of the Palestinians and make it unclear to an Israeli eye.

Another Israeli response did suggest attentive listening to his/her Palestinian interlocutors. The respondent stated that some Palestinians want more normal, routine lives and peace, just as Israelis do, while some want 'revenge, occupation [of Israel] and the deportation of Israelis from the Middle East.' He/she went on: 'The majority are interested in peace and in the Israeli acknowledgement of the crimes committed against Palestinian people, allowing free movement, free living and the right of return...'

The Israeli responses to the question 'What do the Israelis want now?' in 2013 conveyed not only an understanding of, but also a measure of empathy with, the range of positions across the Israeli spectrum. Respondents varied in terms of the positions they attributed to 'most' and 'some' Israelis.

By 2016, however, their responses conveyed a greater detachment, simply describing the different Israeli camps and then focusing criticism on those who justify their hard-line stance on the basis of disbelief in 'the Palestinian narrative', if not actual denial of the Palestinian people. Two respondents voiced a sense of foreboding about the rise of Israeli hardliners, while another depicted the dominance of those who prefer the status quo or inertia, given the seeming impossibility of reaching agreement or finding a way to break the impasse.

Palestinian Participants

When asked 'What do the Palestinians want now?' in November 2013 the Palestinian Olive Tree participants prioritised attainment of Palestinian rights. As one summarised:

> Palestinians want a country. Palestinians want their rights back, and Palestinians want equality, at least. Palestinians want justice, Palestinians want to be heard more, noticed more. Palestinians want to be recognized.

Others mentioned the Right of Return, and one said some want war, but most just want to feed their families. A single respondent answered: 'I don't know'!

In effect they started out with a list of all the positive things the Palestinians want, but by the finish, in July 2016, they were also clear about what they do not want. As one put it: 'In the end all Palestinians want to live a life free of violence, war, internal and international turmoil'. Several also still called for the Right of Return and they would have been well aware of the consequences for Jewish Israelis of the exercise of this right.

I conjecture, therefore, that mixed in with anger about what they lack compared with the Israelis, there was no compunction about repeating a demand that frightens Israelis. There was some speculation on the paucity of incentives for Israel to end Palestinian suffering and the challenge that Palestinian independence and freedom would pose for Israel. As one said:

Giving the Palestinians their rights or a state means the end of the state of Israel. So, there is no peace on the horizon. But who knows, I could be wrong.

Yet, to deduce that the respondents had a 'zero-sum' assessment of the situation does not seem to capture adequately the entirety of what they were saying. To better discern their meaning perhaps the responses to this question need to be seen in conjunction with their responses to other questions, notably the next one: What do the Israelis want now?

In 2013 the most measured Palestinian response to this question was: 'They want peace but by that they mean no more Palestinian resistance while they take more and more'. Other responses emphasised the seeming insatiability of Israeli aspirations. For example:

I can only say that the Israelis are not looking for a peaceful outcome in the region, and their very messed up convictions of their Jewish identity will always want more and more to possess and occupy, therefore they will always try to make their illusionist 'Jewish state' from the Nile to the Euphrates river happen.

Another mentioned the expulsion of the Palestinians as one of the things the Israelis want.

In 2016, the balance of views was that the Israelis want the Palestinians to put up with the occupation and drop all resistance, or else miraculously disappear. This is a departure from the early emphasis on Israeli expansionism and places the emphasis on what the Israelis want vis a vis the Palestinians. This line reflects what the 5th Cohort Israelis also thought about their own society and told the Palestinians.

———

It is easy to become confused when immersed in the detail of the different Israeli and Palestinian depictions of their own society and the other. In a way, that is how it should be, to gain an insight into the lived experience of the protagonists. What is clear, however, is that both the Palestinians and Israelis are the experts on themselves. But, in the absence of anything better than their respective experiences of 'the facts on the ground' they can only *theorise* about the other – they do not actually know them.

If exposed to intensive contact with counterparts from the other side, however, they do gain new information, new knowledge, albeit not necessarily very palatable. While in London, the Olive Tree participants experienced a level of equality with one another which contrasts with the structural inequality that defines their relations 'back home'. They also had a chance to explain themselves and listen to their counterparts which is not possible on the ground, in the conflict zone.

The significance of this exposure can be understood if juxtaposed with something one of my Israeli friends revealed to me years ago. He told me that if it is your job, while serving in the IDF, to preside at one of the checkpoints in the occupied territories, you find yourself taking part in the daily humiliation of Palestinians wishing to pass through. After a while, he said, you start to hate the people who 'make you' humiliate them. As a functionary in a system that you cannot easily opt out of, your capacity to exercise personal choice or take an individual stand is limited, unless you are willing to risk becoming an outcast.

There are plenty of examples of Israelis and Palestinians choosing to see the other as people like themselves and treat them accordingly, but by going against the general grain of their respective national narratives they pay a price. Such narratives, by their very nature, tell us what it means to be us and imbue us with values that distinguish between what is noble and patriotic and what is cowardly or disloyal. They also provide us with a characterisation of the enemy which is actually a rationalisation of our own emotional reactions to that enemy, rather than an assessment based on direct acquaintance and attentive listening.

It is not uncommon, therefore, to find highly educated and thoughtful Israelis who assert that the Palestinians have 'a culture of violence' that forces Israeli society in general to be defensive and for ever on guard. Take the name of the Israeli armed forces, for example, which is the Israel Defence Forces. And look at the general pattern of the Israeli responses to my survey questions, which, along with caveats and regret, disallow trusting *some* Palestinians for fear of the belligerent others.

Meanwhile, among the Palestinians, their responses to my questions indicate that in their narrative also their depiction of the other is a rationalisation of their emotional reactions to the constraints placed upon them. As so many of them insisted in the survey, the Israelis must *want* to subjugate and punish them, otherwise how else to explain their actions?

Trouble is, this may not be a total misrepresentation. After all, it is to be expected that anyone in the role of occupier would prefer that to being one of the occupied. Also, a position of superiority can be habit-forming. The Israeli writer David Grossman has even ventured the opinion that Israelis have become 'addicted' to the occupation, as in addicted to exercising superiority.[12]

It is in this sense that I see the national narratives as drivers which are progressively deepening the conflict and entrapping both communities into cycles of mutual hostility. I also cannot see how 'the facts on the ground' can be seen in isolation from the parallel narratives. The two are intertwined, and the parallel narratives seek to make sense of the 'facts' in contrasting ways. Plus, the narratives contain within them characterisations of 'the other' which self-perpetuate.

The cross-conflict dialogue pursued within the Olive Tree Programme did enable at least some participants to attain new knowledge, in particular about the power of the narratives and their role in reinforcing a status quo that the Palestinians abhor. Israeli participants in the dialogue found it difficult to reconcile this realisation with their personal desire to be 'good people'. The net result, for both sides, was discomfort and frustration. Without a real commitment at the political leadership level to redress the inequalities in bilateral relations, ordinary people are effectively trapped.

As it turned out, many of the Olive Tree Israelis came away from the Programme with a sense of obligation to do what they could to awaken their fellow countrymen and women to the reality that had dawned on they themselves. Several of them went on to work for organisations dedicated to improving the human rights conditions of the Palestinians. A few previously obedient IDF reserve officers refused to engage in combat when the next hot war loomed. They deserve recognition for their courage in going against the grain of the prevailing Israeli national narrative, but it will take more than their individual examples to change minds on a grand scale.

For their part, many Palestinians came away feeling some sense of achievement that they had helped at least a few Israelis see the occupation more objectively. They also came to value these Israelis as friends, in so far as they refused call-up for reserve duty thereafter or, went on to work for change in other ways.

---

[12] Grossman voiced this view in a conversation with David Hare that is included in the latter's animation 'Wall'.

The Olive Tree dialogue was therefore not an exercise in 'normalisation' of the status quo, quite the contrary. To repeat my earlier point, however, what one exceptional exercise in dialogue cannot do, even if replicated several times, is make peace on a grand scale. As discussed in Chapter 1, to expect that would be absurd. Only a fundamental change at the leadership level can do that.

6
The Peace Business and 'Oslo' in Particular

Thus far in this study the focus has been mostly on the two main protagonists in the Israeli-Palestinian conflict, how they see themselves and each other. Yet they, and their conflict, do not exist in a vacuum. On the contrary, at no point in the evolution of the conflict have the two parties been left entirely to their own devices and various *other* actors have been and continue to be involved. While purporting to be primarily interested in helping to bring about peace in the Middle East, these actors have different visions of peace which reveal their preoccupations with material issues and aversion to thinking deeply about the narrative drivers of conflict that are featured in this work.

Having first set the scene and provided some background, in particular about the so-called 'Oslo process', this chapter will examine the ways in which the various regional and international actors are portrayed by the participants in the survey exercise conducted for this study. As will be seen, all the respondents in that survey identified several outsiders as involved in the story but differed on the extent to which they held these players responsible for the trajectory of the conflict *and* the 'peace process'. Respondents were asked to comment in particular on the legacy of 'the Oslo process' and while the Palestinians had very strong and largely negative views on this, the Israelis generally viewed it more positively, as discussed below.

An attempt is also made here to illustrate how the national or group narratives of the *external* actors have shaped their perspectives on the conflict and their preferences for its resolution. My assessment is that, for the most part, the external actors have depicted their own attempts at conflict resolution as broadly reasonable and practical and they have blamed one or both of the protagonists for lack of progress. In other words, they have been as prone to 'othering,' or particularising foreigners and cultures different to their own, as have the Israelis and Palestinians. That said, among those representatives of 'the international community' who have been most engaged *on the ground*, there has been awareness of flaws in both the design and the implementation of successive peace initiatives.

The International Dimensions of the Conflict

As identified by the Israelis and Palestinians surveyed for this work, Zionism had its origins in Europe and was in large part a response to European nationalist movements and discrimination against Jews. The movement received a boost when imperial Britain decided to issue the Balfour Declaration. In so doing, the British hoped to win favour with Jews influential in Washington and thereby help to bring the United States into the First World War on the same side as Britain.[1] The British also wanted control of Palestine to better manage their access to the Suez Canal to the south and to Iraqi and Persian Gulf oil to the north-east.

The League of Nations, formed after the war, gave the Mandates for Palestine and Iraq to Britain. In so doing, it incorporated the Balfour Declaration into the terms of the Mandate for Palestine. Meanwhile, as seen in Chapters 3 and 4, Palestinian nationalism was inspired by broader Arab nationalism that, in turn, grew in response to British (and French) imperialist designs on the Arab world.

Jumping ahead, the horrors of the Holocaust and its legacy were a purely European phenomenon, but with repercussions for the Jews and Arabs in Mandate Palestine. One of its impacts was to reinforce the case for a Jewish 'home' where Jews could be safe. This imperative featured in the thinking of members of the United Nations when, in 1947, they adopted a resolution to partition Palestine between a Jewish state and an Arab one. This was welcomed by the Zionists, who, as also discussed previously, saw it as legitimisation of their aspirations. In rejecting partition, Arab nationalists, including the Palestinians, saw Zionism as a manifestation of European settler colonialism.

In the context of the Cold War, Israel was accorded the support of the Western powers while its Arab opponents were backed by the Soviet Union. The Americans and Soviets were ranged on opposite sides in the 1967 Arab-Israeli war. At the end of the subsequent war in 1973, the United States took the lead in establishing the ceasefire lines.

The efforts of US Secretary of State Henry Kissinger in that regard was one

---

[1] Schneer, J. (2011) *The Balfour Declaration: The Origins of the Israeli-Palestinian Conflict* London: Bloomsbury.

of many US interventions in pursuit of Arab-Israeli peace.[2] Perhaps the most celebrated of these, prior to the 1990s, was that of President Jimmy Carter. He convened the Camp David summit that led to the Egypt-Israel Treaty of 1979. According to Seth Anziska, based on archival research and interviews with key actors, that agreement also set in place the parameters of Palestinian prospects thereafter.[3] Anziska's revealing work is one of the most recent in a long list of authoritative books that have been published on international involvement in the search for a peace agreement between the Israelis and the Palestinians. References to these works appear throughout this book, but, I do not propose to digress into further discussion of them here.

Suffice to say, overall, the Israeli-Palestinian conflict cannot be understood in isolation and external actors have played a role in reinforcing some aspects of the narratives of the protagonists and wilfully ignoring others. They have, unsurprisingly, acted in ways that conformed with their own views of the world and their own self-perceptions and justifications. My purpose in making this observation is to counter the view that the Israeli-Palestinian conflict is somehow uniquely problematic and the protagonists uniquely belligerent or obdurate. On the contrary, I contend, in the way in which they have become trapped in the interplay of their respective narratives they simply provide a demonstration of what can happen when any two or more warring parties spiral ever deeper into conflict. In addition, external actors have used the conflict to play out some of their own agendas, as opposed to being simply impartial mediators.

What *is* unusual about the Israeli-Palestinian conflict, is *the extent* to which both governments and people on the outside have become invested in different outcomes. Governments or states, whether knowingly or not, have demonstrated a preference for the sovereign rights of states in general, over the rights of non-state actors, including resistance movements and insurgencies. The 'rules of the game' in international politics privilege states over revisionist movements. Those who benefit most from the prevailing 'international order' prefer the perpetuation of that order to insurrection. Thus, in so far as the Palestinians in

---

[2] See for example: Touval, S. (1982) *The Peace Brokers: Mediators in the Arab-Israeli Conflict, 1948-1979* Princeton: Princeton University Press, and Miller, A. D. (2008) *The Much Too Promised Land: America's Elusive Search for Arab-Israeli Peace* New York: Bantum Dell.

[3] Anziska, S. (2018) *Preventing Palestine: A Political History from Camp David to Oslo* Princeton and Oxford: Princeton University Press.

general, and PLO leader Yasser Arafat in particular, have been associated with insurgency, guerrilla warfare and terrorism, their quest for national self-determination has been treated with wariness and ambivalence by the status quo powers.

States – foreign governments – are not the only outsiders with a stake in the conflict, however. Human rights campaigners want international humanitarian law upheld wherever and whenever rights are being abused, and for them state actors are often the problem as opposed to the solution. For this constituency Israel has become much more the object of criticism than Palestinian terrorists. Anti-imperialists and revolutionaries champion the Palestinian cause on the grounds that they are oppressed. The campaign for Boycott, Divestment and Sanctions (BDS), inspired by the earlier campaign against apartheid in South Africa, has garnered so much international public support that the Israelis, with supporters in the United States and Europe, have mounted a counter-campaign to outlaw BDS.

In the case of Israel-Palestine, there is also a strong religious dimension. Sites holy to Jews, Christians and Muslims exist in and around Jerusalem, Nazareth and across the West Bank. The adherents of different faiths want to make common cause with their co-religionists and/or defend them. Many differ vehemently within their faith groups over what will and should happen in 'the Holy Land'. In addition to these international connections, Jews and Palestinians around the world have relatives in Israel and Palestine and care very much for their safety.

In many ways, therefore, there is a tendency on the part of outsiders to almost *over*-identify with one or other of the protagonists in the Israeli-Palestinian conflict. To add to the complications, it has come to be seen as a sort of laboratory in which different weapons systems, surveillance technologies and security doctrines can be tested.[4] It is also a setting in which professional diplomats and politicians aspire to hone their negotiating skills and enhance their reputations. Over the years there have been some very big egos involved in the Middle East peace process and the record of their failures seems only to encour-

---

[4] The curriculum for the MA in War Studies at King's College London that I undertook in the 1970s included the study of successive Arab-Israeli wars.

age successor generations to try their hand.[5]

At another level, journalists are drawn to the Israeli-Palestinian conflict as a setting in which to demonstrate their professionalism and show that they can withstand criticism from all quarters.[6] Academic researchers, myself included, want to study the conflict, and have found it easier to access than many other war zones, where it is simply too dangerous for non-native scholars to venture without very serious risk.[7]

Even the Olive Tree Programme itself can be understood as a manifestation of the extent of outside interest in this conflict. It was initiated (before my time as director) by people who wanted to prove that peace is possible and that cross-conflict dialogue can contribute to that. As explained in Chapter 2, the financial investment in making the Olive Tree Programme happen was substantial (approximately £60,000 per participant over three years and not counting staff costs). The sponsors, almost all from the corporate sector, saw it as a 'good cause' and one to be associated with. It is hard to imagine a similar investment of private resources in an initiative to end conflict in the Congo, for example, or to resolve Indian-Pakistani differences over the future of Kashmir.

So, the Israeli-Palestinian conflict attracts extraordinary levels of external interest and not all facets of this can be understood as purely altruistic. Politicians in the United States, Canada and across Europe are fully aware that their policies toward Israel and the Palestinians are under constant scrutiny from domestic lobbies and interest groups. Yet they persist in their efforts to bring it to an end, while also trying to avoid incurring too much criticism of themselves.

Both the Israelis and the Palestinians are also aware of this fascination with their situation. Both welcome the attention in many respects, but also complain bitterly when they think their positions are not being adequately heard or un-

---

[5] For example, US Presidents Carter, Reagan, Clinton and George W. Bush; Secretaries of State Henry Kissinger, James Baker and John Kerry; and British Prime Ministers Margaret Thatcher and Tony Blair.

[6] As explored in Rodgers, J. (2013) *No Road Home: Fighting for Land and Faith in Gaza* Bury St Edmunds, Abramis Academic Publishing; Rodgers, J. (2015) *Headlines from the Holy Land: Reporting the Israeli-Palestinian Conflict* Basingstoke and New York: Palgrave Macmillan; and Harb, Z., ed., (2017) *Reporting the Middle East: The Practice of News in the Twenty-first Century* London: I.B. Tauris.

[7] Increasingly such access has become more difficult, however, as the Israeli authorities have denied visas to some academics, particularly those with Palestinian origins or deemed to be biased in favour of the Palestinians.

derstood. Both want international public opinion on their side and both want external support. By definition, therefore, it is rare for both parties to be satisfied at the same time. Consequently, while often expressing cynicism, both parties continue to believe that the international community can make a difference to their fate, as demonstrated in the responses to the survey questions discussed below and in the next chapter.

Before turning to those survey results, however, there is more scene-setting to do, particularly in relation to the 'Oslo process', since this proved to be such a turning point in the trajectory of the conflict and such a source of contention among the respondents to the survey. The outline summary of the Oslo process that follows is a demonstration of the ways in which various external actors have pursued conflicting agendas of their own. There is an element here of 'too many cooks spoiling the broth!'

The Oslo Process

The genesis of the 'Oslo process' was of course the outline agreement reached between Israeli and Palestinian negotiators in 1992 during back-channel talks convened by the Norwegians. At the time, international attention was focused on formal negotiations in Washington, initiated by the Americans and Russians at the Madrid Conference of 1991. The PLO and its leader Yasser Arafat were excluded from the formal negotiations, though Arafat was kept in the picture by the Palestinian team who were there. What Arafat clearly wanted, however, was more direct involvement, and the Norwegians enabled that by focusing the back channel on reaching an accommodation between Arafat on the one hand and the leading Israeli Labour Party figures Yitzhak Rabin and Shimon Peres on the other.

The resulting agreement was formally adopted by the Americans and President Bill Clinton presided at the signing ceremony on the White House lawn in 1993. Effectively the Americans then 'owned' it, with the blessing of the Norwegians.

From the start there were critics and sceptics. The deal was asymmetrical, in that, while the PLO recognised Israel, in return Israel simply recognised the PLO. It was nonetheless a breakthrough since, as the Europeans had been saying since their Venice Declaration of 1980, the PLO needed to be involved in the quest for peace. As the Europeans had also been arguing for years, the right of the Palestinians to self-determination had to be recognised. What the

Europeans had not said, however, was what that might mean. They, as too the Americans, for the whole of the 1990s, insisted that only direct negotiations between the Israeli and PLO leaders could determine what shape self-determination should take.

In recognising Israel, the PLO leaders assumed they were recognising pre-1967 Israel, excluding East Jerusalem, the rest of the West Bank and the Gaza Strip. They expected those areas, which Israel had captured in the '67 war, to become the Palestinian state. What the Israelis assumed was that they had simply agreed to negotiate, with the PLO, over what and how much Israel would relinquish in those territories. The most hopeful Israelis and Palestinians saw in Oslo the makings of a viable two state solution to the conflict. The most cynical, or perhaps one might say the most calculating, saw Oslo as a way for Israel to control the Palestinians more effectively.[8] For the most part, the various external players simply wanted Oslo to end the conflict – by mutual agreement – which in practice meant satisfying the Israelis while keeping the Palestinians on board.

Oslo I was followed up with Oslo II (in 1995). In combination, these accords established that the Palestinians would elect a Palestinian Authority (PA) – an executive presidency and a legislature – to have autonomous control of civil administration and internal security in Palestinian cities (Area A), that is 4-5 percent of the West Bank plus Gaza. In a further 23 per cent or so of the West Bank (Area B) the PA would have similar internal powers, but conduct security operations jointly with the Israelis. The rest of the occupied territories (Area C) would remain under full Israeli control pending the outcome of further negotiations.

Oslo anticipated that the 'final status issues', namely: borders, Jerusalem, refugees, security, water and, crucially, sovereignty, would be negotiated between the parties within a five-year time frame during which 'confidence-building' measures would enhance cooperation and build the trust required to reach a final deal. In fact, the Israelis and Palestinians spent almost all those five years implementing the interim arrangements. The assassination of Rabin in November 1995 by an Israeli extremist was a major setback and in 1996 Labour was replaced in government by Likud and Binyamin Netanyahu became Prime Minister for the first time. He was not enthusiastic about the Oslo process.

---

[8] Anziska, S. (2018) *Preventing Palestine: A Political History from Camp David to Oslo* Princeton and Oxford: Princeton University Press, p.5.

Sporadic acts of violence by Palestinians and some by Israelis, continued overall control of Palestinian movements by Israeli forces, plus the continued growth of Jewish settlements in the West Bank, meant that people on both sides increasingly harboured doubts that the whole process could really deliver. There were some who did not want it to.[9]

During this period not only the Americans, but also the European Union and its members states, plus other international 'donors' such as Japan, Canada, Switzerland and the Norwegians, committed unprecedented amounts of aid and numerous personnel to supporting the process. There were grand plans for infrastructure development, including a port and airport in Gaza. The airport was built, but subsequently closed. When the PA was accused of corruption, the Europeans and the World Bank instituted measures to keep its operations transparent and accountable. Other donor country initiatives included the people-to-people activities discussed in Chapter 1.

Yasser Arafat welcomed the investment but chafed at controls. His constituency ran beyond the West Bank and Gaza to the refugees in neighbouring countries among whom he had lived and orchestrated guerrilla operations against Israel in the 1960s, '70s and '80s. The newly created Palestinian police forces, trained and equipped by the international donors, included members of Arafat's retinue from his time in exile, who did not always work well with local Palestinians. Ordinary Palestinians complained about personal rivalries, favouritism and corruption inside the rank and file of the PA and its security forces. A divide had been opened up between the Palestinian insiders and outsiders.[10] International attention was focused on obtaining a deal between Israel and the

---

[9] From my vantage point as Head of the Middle East Programme, first at the Royal United Services Institute (RUSI) from 1990-95 and then at the Royal Institute of International Affairs (Chatham House) I monitored the twists and turns in the Oslo process. With respect to the international players, Western politicians and diplomats were swift to refute any of us 'experts' who voiced concerns about its prospects. For example, I recollect one British Ambassador to the region telling me, 'failure is not an option'; and a British Labour MP berating me for underrating its prospects. Her conviction was that Oslo could be *made* to work provided we abandoned all doubts.

[10] During the course of a project I ran with a Lebanese colleague at Chatham House, focusing on the Palestinian refugee issue, we convened several meetings between refugee representatives and Arab host-country nationals. Those Palestinian participants, including refugees, who came from inside the West Bank and Gaza, had heated arguments with refugees from Lebanon, Syria and Jordan over priorities. The latter did not want their rights to be sidelined in the quest for statehood in the West Bank and Gaza.

PA, headed by Arafat, while leaving the refugee question on hold.

Built into the whole Oslo concept was the expectation that the Palestinians would have to earn their hoped-for state by demonstrating that they would no longer represent a threat to Israel and Israeli security. The donor community, and particularly the Americans and Europeans, kept telling the Palestinians, in effect, that the better they behaved the more likely they were to achieve their goals. The credibility of this implicit promise waned, as, especially during Netanyahu's premiership in the 1990s, no progress was made on the final status negotiations and settlement expansion increased. Repeatedly, the more obdurate Netanyahu became, the more the international players urged the Palestinians to go further to meet Israeli security concerns, or themselves worked to find ways around the problems.[11] European room for manoeuvre was in any case limited by US insistence that Washington retain control of the political process while the EU keep providing the funds.

When Labour returned to power in Israel and Ehud Barak replaced Netanyahu as Prime Minister in 1999, the year the final status negotiations were supposed to have been completed, Barak and the Clinton administration focused initially on negotiations with the Syrians. Only when these failed[12] did attention focus again on the Israeli-Palestinian track. By this time Israeli security officials were warning that Palestinian frustration was nearing boiling point. So Clinton and Barak decided to go for a make-or-break summit at Camp David in July 2000. It was a disaster.

In their retrospectives on what went wrong, two US officials intimately involved in the quest for peace during the Clinton administration, Dennis Ross and Aaron David Miller, gave two very different assessments. In his published accounts of the Oslo years, Ross found fault with the approaches of all the key players. But he held Palestinian leader Yasser Arafat most to blame for the failure at Camp David and its aftermath. Looking back in 2002, Ross told Fox News:

---

[11] For several well-informed views on this aspect of the process see Keating, M., Anne Le More and Robert Lowe, eds., (2005) *Aid, Diplomacy and Facts on the Ground: The Case of Palestine* London: Chatham House.

[12] Rabinovich, I. (1998) *The Brink of Peace: The Israeli-Syrian Negotiations* Princeton: Princeton University Pres; and Lesch, D. (2008) *The Arab-Israeli Conflict: A History* Oxford: Oxford University Press, pp.366-69.

Arafat's whole life has been governed by struggle and a cause. Everything he has done as leader of the Palestinians is to always leave his options open, never close a door. He was being asked here, you've got to close the door. For him to end the conflict is to end himself.[13]

Ross then conjectured that Arafat encouraged the outbreak of the second Intifada in the belief that more violence would pressure the Israelis and the Americans to offer more. He then added:

You have to understand that [Israeli Prime Minister Ehud] Barak was able to reposition Israel internationally. Israel was seen as having demonstrated unmistakably it wanted peace, and the reason it wasn't available, achievable, was because Arafat wouldn't accept it. Arafat needed to re-establish the Palestinians as a victim, and unfortunately they are a victim, and we see it now in a terrible way.[14]

In his appraisal of what went wrong, Aaron David Miller arrived at a very different assessment. In a book he published in 2008 Miller wrote:

Toward the end of Camp David there was a serious discussion of a 'partial deal' that would have deferred Jerusalem. But for most of Camp David's thirteen days, Barak wouldn't hear of it. Once Jerusalem became a focal point, Arafat had to fight to defend Arab rights there and couldn't accept an agreement without it.[15]

He went on:

Once the summit ended, Barak's make-or-break mindset faded. In late September, before the outbreak of the second Intifada, he would have his best meeting with Arafat ever, and negotiations continued; Barak and his

---

[13] https://www.washingtoninstitute.org/policy-analysis/view/the-aftermath-of-camp-da-vid-2000

[14] Ibid.

[15] Miller, Aaron David (2008) *The Much Too Promised Land: America's Elusive Search for Arab-Is-raeli Peace* New York: Bantum Dell, p.307.

non-existent redlines continued to move toward Palestinian positions. At the same time Barak blamed Arafat for the summit's failure and cajoled an already sympathetic Clinton into doing the same.[16]

While Barak and Clinton's anger were understandable, Miller conceded, he could not help thinking that: 'our behaviour in blaming the Palestinians and facilitating Barak's campaign to delegitimize Arafat as a partner was immature and counterproductive.' As it transpired, the Clinton administration went on dealing with Arafat and by the end of 2000, in the midst of the second Intifada and just before he left office, Clinton tabled his 'parameters' for a deal which went far further than the ideas floated at Camp David had done to address Palestinian concerns. The so-called Taba talks, in early 2001, concluded with an outline 'two-state' deal.

By that point, however, such momentum as had been achieved was lost, not least because Clinton had reached the end of his second term in office and the incoming President George W. Bush was not minded to pick up where his predecessor had left off. Crucially also Ehud Barak was replaced by Ariel Sharon in the election of February 2001. Sharon would have nothing to do with Arafat, characterising him as a terrorist and, in the face of the second Intifada Sharon masterminded the campaign which nearly destroyed the PA, reinstated Israeli military control in the West Bank and Gaza Strip, and started construction of the security barrier discussed in the last chapter.

It was only thanks to the EU that the PA did not collapse totally. European diplomats said at the time that they had to keep the PA afloat to counter Sharon's argument that he had no Palestinian partner for peace. The EU also decided to actually name a 'two-state solution' to the conflict as its preferred outcome for the peace process, but even then, they stipulated that this would have to come about by agreement between Israel and the Palestinians. Sharon preferred to pursue a unilateral approach, including withdrawing Israeli settlements and the IDF from inside the Gaza Strip in 2005. Despite pleas from UN, American and European officials, this withdrawal was not coordinated with the PA and militants in Gaza resorted to renewed violent resistance against Israel. The Israeli response included reinstatement of controls on Gaza which impeded plans for rebuilding its economy.

---

[16] Ibid.

The high point in the development of an international consensus on a pre-ferred formula for ending the Israeli-Palestinian conflict came in this context. In March 2002, the UN Security Council adopted a resolution that spelled out the objective of a 'two-state solution.'[17] A month later the so-called Quartet – made up of the UN, the United States, Russia and the EU – was formally es-tablished to coordinate on the realisation of their goal. The same year the Arab League adopted an initiative pledging to recognise Israel provided it withdrew from the territories it had occupied in 1967 and agree to accept the return of at least some refugees, among other stipulations.

In 2003 the Quartet launched the so-called Roadmap[18] for realisation of the 'two-state solution' in stages, but US President Bush announced that he did not expect the Israelis to relinquish *all* of the West Bank territory it had occupied in 1967. Crucially, the Roadmap required both the Israelis and the Palestinians to abide by a series of stipulations and agree the parameters of a final deal by negotiation. Consequently, as had happened with 'the Oslo process' in the 1990s, the success of the Quartet initiative depended on how the steps toward a final deal were implemented on the ground and on the commitment of the protagonists to eventually reach a mutually acceptable agreement.

In the end, the Quartet failed to make the Roadmap put the 'peace process' back on track. The Americans made another effort to revive it with the so-called Annapolis initiative, which also foundered. After the Bush administration was replaced by that of Barack Obama, his officials tried again, initially calling for a settlement freeze to prepare the ground, which proved only temporary and par-tial. The very last serious US intervention came in Obama's second term, when his Secretary of State John Kerry tried shuttle diplomacy between the parties. In April 2014 Kerry pronounced his initiative at an end. He laid more blame on Israeli intransigence than on Palestinian obduracy. That moment was cause for gloom among the participants in the Olive Tree dialogue in 2014. As one of the Israelis put it, keeping hope alive, even just one percent of hope, is a world away from no hope at all! To counter that, however, a Palestinian made the point that 'despair is not a plan!'

---

[17] In UNSC Resolution 1397 the Council 'affirmed a vision of a region where two States, Israel and Palestine, live side by side within secure and recognized borders.' www.un.org/press/en/2002/sc7326.doc.htm.

[18] http://www.un.org/News/dh/mideast/roadmap122002.pdf

In any case, the legacy of Oslo was Palestinian autonomy in Gaza and parts of the West Bank, the creation of the PA (patched back together after the second Intifada was crushed) and a Palestinian police force charged with keeping order in the territories over which it had some control. From 2007 the Gaza Strip came under the control of Hamas and under Israeli blockade. No new Palestinian elections have been held since.

With the advent of the Trump administration, US commitment to the two-state goal has waned. Trump made the decision to move the US embassy to Israel from Tel Aviv to Jerusalem, leading Palestinian President Mahmoud Abbas to refuse to continue peace negotiations. Latterly the Trump administration has closed the Palestinian representative office in Washington and Congress has cut all US aid to the PA, to UNRWA and to Palestinian NGOs.

Even before these developments, the record shows that neither the Americans nor the Europeans have been bold enough to fully *own* their roles in the genesis and persistence of the conflict. More crucially, in their strategies these external players became so intricately embroiled in the minutiae of mechanisms and institutions invented in the Oslo years that they lost sight of the big picture. The significance of identity issues and competing narratives was downplayed or dismissed as too complex to address. In his assessment, former UN official Michael Keating recorded:

> A great source of frustration for many aid actors is a sense that they have been complicit in, and used to support, diplomatic reluctance to face the facts, and they have not done enough to compel their political masters to do so.[19]

He has also pointed out that: 'Aid flows cannot fill the void created by the absence of a political horizon'; and claimed that: 'Chequebook diplomacy does not work'.[20]

As will now be demonstrated, the legacy of indefinite limbo created by Oslo no longer looks like a step on the road to peace – at least as far as those surveyed for this study are concerned. In the following sections I offer a sum-

---

[19] Keating, M., Anne Le More and Robert Lowe, eds., (2005) *Aid, Diplomacy and Facts on the Ground: The Case of Palestine* London: Chatham House, p.3.

[20] Ibid., p.4.

mary, with illustrations, of the responses of Israelis and Palestinians surveyed in 2016, to the questions: 'Are there any other actors/parties involved in the conflict?' 'If so, who are they and what was their role over time?' and 'Did the Oslo Peace Process fail? If yes, why? If not, what did it achieve?'

Again, I should repeat the caveats previously stipulated and I refer the reader to Chapter 2, pages 48-51 for the full details of the survey undertaken.

Israeli Views on other actors/parties involved in the conflict

When asked the question: 'Are there any other actors/parties involved in the conflict?' all eight non-Olive Tree or 'comparator group' Israeli respondents answered with a 'Yes' except for one, who answered:

> Not significantly, but in the background there are states such as Jordan and Egypt which do carry weight in some areas. Movements such as the Muslim Brotherhood and Jewish diaspora movements can also influence politics and the distribution of resources, in a manner which benefits the side they support.

That respondent dated the origins of the conflict to the 2nd Aliya and Jewish-Arab clashes, making no mention of the British Mandate.

Of the other seven non-Olive Tree Israeli respondents, five answered the question with a simple 'Yes' and one elaborated thus: 'The European states, the United States and the Arab states.' The remaining respondent said: 'Yes: Religious people, the Arab states, Britain, France, the US, the Soviet Union, NGOs.'[21]

Of the fourteen Israeli Olive Tree alumni respondents, all of them answered the question in the affirmative and eight elaborated briefly as follows:

1. There are many other actors involved in the conflict – from the Imperialist European states who divided the land of the Middle East – to the Arab states who fought against Israel – and to Nazi Germany – who

---

[21] Note: the Israeli government has accused the EU among others of interfering in internal Israeli affairs through their funding of Israeli NGOs – targeting only those with a human rights agenda (not foreign funding of settlements) and has passed legislation aimed at limiting the activities of such NGOs.

irreversibly proved to the world that Jews are not safe in exile.

2. British and European Christians, Americans and others, who have an interest in keeping this Middle Eastern piece of land in white hands.
3. Yes. The international community, headed by the US, the Arab states, Britain and the European Union.
4. Definitely, a variety of actors.
5. The conflict was formed as a long-lasting conflict because of the involvement of multiple actors.
6. Western Powers and Arab Countries.
7. Secondary involvement – the neighbouring Arab states and the super-powers. They have very limited influence over the progression of the conflict and its solution.
8. Yes. The actors I will name in [*answer to*] the next question only represent a few selected examples, but the powers influencing the conflict are too many to count.

Not just this last respondent, but all of them, Olive Tree and non-Olive Tree, elaborated on their initial responses in their answers to my follow-up question, which was: 'If so, who are they and what was their role over time?' What they said manifested a range of views, with an emphasis on those actors deemed responsible *for fomenting* the conflict.

As noted above, one respondent mentioned only Jordan and Egypt. By contrast, another respondent volunteered:

All the nations who controlled Palestine throughout history and dictated the settlement and immigration laws – the Ottoman Empire, the British during the Mandate. Nazi Germany – that created the conditions for a mass Jewish immigration to Palestine, intensified the Jewish people's feelings that they need their own nation state, and that plays a major role in the creation of the Israeli ethos until today. The Arab states that took part in wars with Israel, mediated reconciliation attempts, imposed sanctions etc. The states supporting Israel politically and economically, especially the United States. The UN, UNRWA and the European Union that determine policy regarding Israel and Palestine. Organisations and charities supporting both sides.

Other responses may be encapsulated thus: the British because they fomented the Jewish-Arab conflict until it became too costly for them to stay; a series of states from those perpetrating pogroms to imperialists, to superpowers and Europe, to Arab states – in both negative and positive (peace-making) roles; Europe, the US and Arab states; the mixed role of the British during the Mandate and Arab states without whom Palestinian nationalism would not have developed so strongly (others are significant but not in the origins of the conflict); Arabs, Britain, France, US, and Russia who have 'used the Israeli-Palestinian conflict, more than once, as part of their international dealings and considerations'; and, today, the BDS.

There were no major differences between the Olive Tree and non-Olive Tree Israeli responses. However, the Olive Tree respondents had some refinements on the pattern of responses overall. These included: Britain and the Arab states who betrayed/made use of the Palestinians; white Westerners with an imperialist agenda; those giving preferential treatment to Israel; anti-Semites, leading to Zionism and Israel, plus supporters of both sides [in the conflict]; the Diasporas of the two nations; those paying 'lip-service' to the Palestinian cause.

On balance, I would say that the Olive Tree alumni indicated a more negative view of external involvement than did the non-Olive Tree respondents.

Palestinians Views on other actors/parties involved in the conflict

All the Palestinian respondents, Olive Tree and non-Olive Tree, affirmed the involvement of other actors/parties in the origins of the conflict. Those named by the non-Olive Tree respondents included: Arab countries (Egypt was cited as an example) involved by their silence and complicity in 'what Israel is doing'; other countries involved 'through providing Israel with weapons and money' (with the US and France singled out as examples); the British because 'they started the problem'; Jordan, in particular King Abdullah I, because 'he could have liberated us and didn't'; UN members – 'who voted for Israel not us'; the 'House of Saud'; and Germany through its desire 'to atone for the Holocaust'.

One non-Olive Tree respondent also chose to talk about the 'local complicity' of NGOs who 'agree to sign the USAID's document condemning terrorism' [as a condition for receiving aid]. In this he/she was referring to a regulation introduced by the United States requiring all aid recipients to guarantee that none of the funds would end up in the hands of those either using terrorism or supporting the use of terrorism. This measure could be interpreted very strictly, by members of the US Congress, to rule out aid to any body which could not prove that it would only be used for purposes deemed conducive to peace by the US authorities. (By 2018, as noted above, *all* US aid to Palestinian organisations was cut off.)

Another non-Olive Tree respondent noted that, 'after Britain and France came the US' – but was unclear on whether Israel was the pawn or the manipulator in its dealings with these powers.

In the discussion which accompanied the answers to this question from the non-Olive Tree 'comparator group', several respondents wanted to highlight their personal sense of insecurity and the general atmosphere of insecurity that affected them and their families/children.

The responses of the Palestinian Olive Tree alumni broadly echoed those of the non-Olive Tree respondents, accusing Arab countries of neglect and thence complicity, but focusing on the roles of the Western countries: the British, because of Balfour, the Mandate and foundation of Israel; European colonialism (including Hitler); the US and others in the West who let the conflict endure; and overall those who either support Israel, or do not support the Palestinians or both. The word 'complicity' came up repeatedly.

Mention was also made of the UN, for the 'unfair Partition Plan'; foreign complicity with the Palestinian Authority; Germany because of the Holocaust; and those providing weapons, economic and political support to Israel. Some respondents depicted exploitation and perpetuation of the conflict to serve outside interests. According to one alumnus:

> There is one party that is losing from all of this and that's the Palestinian people. We suffer the dirty and depressing consequences that are destroying our lives, future and history.

In all their answers the Olive Tree alumni gave less emphasis than the non-Olive Tree respondents to the daily sense of insecurity and danger at a personal level – emphasising instead their lack of freedom and rights.

How Views evolved among Dialogue Participants

Israeli Participants

Turning to the longtitudinal survey results,[22] all the Israeli respondents answered yes to the question about the involvement of external actors in the conflict in 2013 and again in 2016. In 2013 these 5th Cohort Olive Tree Israelis listed the British Empire, Arab states, the US, Egypt, Jordan, Syria, Lebanon (Sykes-Picot and the Partition Plan), and Soviet-US rivalry. One volunteered that he/she saw the conflict as a continuation of World Wars I and II.

In 2016 their lists included: the Ottomans, Britain, France, the Arab states, the US, the EU and Nazi Germany. As one respondent volunteered initially, his/her awareness of the British role derived from material discussed in various Olive Tree meetings (including public ones like the Olive Tree Middle East Forum and in a closed meeting with the lawyer-writer Zeina Ghandour whose work on the British Mandate was quoted in Chapter 5). It is perhaps worth noting here that a disproportionate amount of time in the Olive Tree activities was devoted to discussing foreign involvement *in the early days* of the conflict, as opposed to more recent times. However, Olive Tree activities did also incorporate simulations and scenario-building exercises, looking at contemporary times and in which both the main protagonists and external actors featured.

When asked to explain the roles of external actors in the conflict over time, *in the beginning*, in 2013, the Israeli responses demonstrated awareness of the Balfour Declaration, conflicting British promises, the carve up of the Middle East after World War I (which made the conflict a feature of regional developments) and decisions during British Mandate rule that contributed to frictions between Jews and Arabs in Palestine. Anti-Semitism in Europe and the UN Partition Plan were also mentioned.

At the end, in 2016, the Israeli responses were not vastly different, but provided much more detail and apportioned some blame, to European anti-Semitism, Western support for Zionism, and the bellicosity of Arab states. For example, one respondent blamed 'the states of Europe that pushed for establishing a Jewish state without considering the existing inhabitants' and another said the Arabs' declaration of war (in 1948) 'granted the Jews a sort of legitimacy to fight the Palestinians despite the fact that most of them were unarmed and did not

---

[22] Explained in Chapter 2.

fight against the IDF".

What was missing at the beginning and the end was much consideration of the more contemporary roles of either the US or the EU. There were no mentions of Iran (and its nuclear programme – which Netanyahu has consistently highlighted in recent years – or its support for Hamas and Hezbollah, for example) nor of the Arab states (and their complicity in the continuation of the occupation) – so often mentioned in Palestinian narratives. Oslo was also not mentioned.

Palestinian Participants

When asked: 'Are there any other actors/parties involved in the origins of the conflict?' the answer from the 5th Cohort Palestinians was 'Yes' in all cases. In the initial responses, of November 2013, the only actors mentioned were the British Empire, the Europeans more generally, and the UN (for partition). By the finish, in July 2016, the list had been extended to also include the US, Egypt, Jordan, Syria, Lebanon.

To the follow-up question: 'If so, who are they and what was their role over time?' *the initial responses* referred to those involved 'by complicity' in the occupation and 'support' for Israel. Europeans were charged with persecution of the Jews and Britain was blamed for crushing Arab uprisings in Mandate Palestine. One respondent said the UN partition 'obviously made the Arabs reject the suggested plan'. The emphasis was all on involvement in the origins of the conflict not the contemporary scene.

In their final responses, the 5th Cohort Palestinians mentioned the suppliers of weapons to Israel, with which to kill Palestinians, and support for Israel in denying the Palestinians their rights. The responses focused on those actors deemed to have helped or contributed to the suffering of the Palestinians. They made no mention of the Arab-Israeli wars, or Iran or the Lebanon wars. They made no mention of PLO relations with the Arab states or Russia. Commenting on what he/she perceived to be the motives for foreign interference, one respondent claimed: 'The goal is to distract and exhaust the concerned parties and the Palestinians without the need for foreign intervention' – an essentially neo-imperialist argument.

By the finish, therefore, more emphasis was evident on the US role in arming and supporting Israel and the neglect of the Arab states, with both therefore enabling the occupation to continue.

Israeli Perspectives on the Oslo Peace Process

When asked the question: 'Did the Oslo Peace Process fail? If yes, why? If not, what did it achieve?' all but one of the non-Olive Tree Israeli respondents declared it a partial success. The one exception saw it as changing the parameters of the conflict and as 'brave and visionary', but ultimately failing 'because nothing was solved as of yet, and each second that passes further fans and inflames the sturdy roots of the conflict'. This person attributed the failure of Oslo to its designation of the 1967 border as the basis for a deal, when, in his/her view, this was insufficient to satisfy all the Palestinian aspirations and beyond what Israelis could or would concede.

For the rest of the non-Olive Tree Israeli respondents, however, Oslo not only demonstrated that agreement was possible between the protagonists, even if not yet fully realised, but also produced some positive gains for both parties. This response exemplifies the majority non-Olive Tree Israeli assessment:

> The Oslo process failed partially. In terms of the final product which was supposed to emerge as a result of the process – an independent Palestinian state alongside a Jewish democratic state – it is obvious that this goal was not met and that, in this respect, the process failed. However, the process cannot be defined as a total failure because of the establishment of the Palestinian Authority (an accomplishment) which represents the Palestinian people and which forms an entity that Israel can coordinate security arrangements with and negotiate with when it is possible. Another successful product of the process was the division of the Palestinian territory into areas A, B and C. In area A, at least, the Palestinians have full municipal and governmental independence.

Turning to the responses of the Israeli Olive Tree alumni, they identified pluses (the creation of the PA) and minuses (no peace) in the Olso process. They reflected that, by signing Oslo, the Israelis did acknowledge that the pre-Oslo status quo was not viable and recognized the Palestinian people. Yet it brought no end to the violence and, according to one, it failed because the Israeli government and its supporters were against it. Another alumnus blamed both leaderships; and another said Oslo 'parked the problem' which was detrimental to peace. In the words of one Israeli Olive Tree alumnus:

The process failed in some respects and succeeded in others. It failed because it did not manage to lead to a permanent agreement with the Palestinians, an agreement which will bring the conflict with the Palestinians to an end. It succeeded because it gave the Palestinians autonomy and released Israel from the need to run the daily lives of Palestinians in many aspects. It also paved the way to what could one day become a Palestinian state.

Another made this assessment:

The Oslo process failed because it did not demand the dismantlement of the settlements. It failed because political powers, headed by the Israeli right and Prime Minister Netanyahu, did not want the process to take place. It failed because the destructive terrorist attacks, in the hearts of Israeli cities, realised their objectives and scared the Israelis. The achievement of the process is the mutual recognition between Israel and the PLO. Another achievement is the creation of a process that was inconceivable beforehand.

Yet another respondent saw a progression in the Israeli nationalist narrative as a key problem:

Over the past 20 years it seems that we have only moved further and further away from reaching some kind of a permanent agreement and, at this point in time, it seems that neither side is interested in performing the compromises necessary for re-launching the peace talks. The Israeli society's discourse (and the way it is reflected by public representatives in Knesset) reflects the strengthening of nationalism, and of the Greater Israel idea, and the deepening of the hatred towards the other in Israeli society. In contrast to the Rabin government and the goals of the Oslo process, this current hawkish government (and the society that elected this government) is more interested in enhancing Israeli control over the territories than beginning a process of sovereignty transfer.

Overall, the Israeli Olive Tree alumni *did* see value in Oslo *because* it recognised the Palestinians and the need for a negotiated peace. As one put it, the failure 'is not absolute, because the Oslo process was a step forward in the sense of public opinion regarding the recognition of the other side's existence and the possibility of a solution for the conflict'. In this respect, the alumni placed more emphasis than the members of the 'comparator group' on the positive value of recognition of 'the other'. The non-Olive Tree Israelis, by contrast, accorded more value to Oslo as a vehicle for managing the problem.

Palestinian Perspectives on the Oslo Peace Process

As explained in Chapter 2 and noted subsequently, the non-Olive Tree Palestinian respondents to the survey answered my questions in a 'focus group' convened by a Palestinian research and polling organisation in Ramallah. The members of that group, fourteen in total, came from three West Bank towns (or nearby villages or refugee camps), namely Tulkarem, Ramallah and Bethlehem. The group was convened to serve as a source of comparison with Palestinian Olive Tree alumni – however, their responses to my questions are obviously of interest in themselves.

This applies in particular to their answers to the questions about the Oslo process and, as discussed later in Chapter 7, their thoughts on 'What should happen now?' They became animated and quite vociferous when discussing Oslo and their verdicts on the Oslo Process were mostly negative, in terms of what it meant for them. 'It didn't achieve anything – for us' said one. It failed because the situation got worse, said most, or else, it worked initially, but then it brought 'poverty, unemployment, checkpoints, settlements and the security situation'. As summarised by one:

> Oslo is a total failure for us, but the Jews are happy with it. We, the Palestinians, don't learn. The Jews will never do anything in our interests. They always act in their own interest. We always go back to negotiations and agreements with them. What was taken by force can only be restored by force. It's all nonsense.

Another of these non-Olive Tree Palestinians said:

> I think the biggest mistake the PLO made was signing Oslo. You can't have security coordination if the two parties are not equal. Israel is stronger than us. They fooled themselves with the security coordination. If there was any hope that countries start supporting us again it's gone now. I think King

Hussein was supporting us in the 1960s. After Oslo everything changed.

And another:

> It didn't achieve anything. It had terrible consequences. It's enough we acknowledged Israel's existence in return for an imaginary national authority. What use is the PA? I defy anyone to say it is the preliminary for a Palestinian state. My ambition is Ramla and Lod, not a Palestinian state. It certainly failed.

Several of them mentioned specific ways in which the Oslo framework had come to constrain rather than increase their freedoms. Their tax receipts could be withheld from the PA by the Israelis. The corridor that was supposed to enable movement between the West Bank and Gaza was never created. The settlements kept expanding and dominating their lives. Also, as illustrated in the last response quoted above, they aspired to far more than Oslo delivered and were disappointed – as suggested by one of the Israeli respondents quoted previously. Many did grant that in the beginning, when Oslo was first signed, there was a general sense of optimism about what it could deliver – but that had long since dissipated.

A number of these respondents also took the opportunity to voice their disappointments with the PA. One said of the PA officials: 'They divide the cake among the returnees and a small group of locals. It all became about cars, houses, villas, jobs and salaries.' Another asked: 'What's the point of Palestinian police officers? When the Israeli army comes to arrest someone they disappear.'

There were some, however, who granted that they preferred to have Palestinian police officers rather than Israeli ones, for day-to-day police work. Many also conceded that Oslo had enabled improvements in the Palestinian school curriculum, which meant Palestinians could now learn about their own national history and cause. One other positive they identified was in terms of medical care, because there was coordination between Palestinian and Israeli hospitals for the treatment of severe cases.

Overall, the responses of the non-Olive Tree Palestinians to the questions about Oslo revealed strongly felt emotions and resentments at the constraints imposed upon them on a daily basis and their sense of deprivation, frustration and loss.

Turning now to the responses of the Olive Tree Palestinian alumni about Oslo, they were less exercised about specifics, but laid even more emphasis on the way the PA had been co-opted for Israeli purposes, as they saw it. With one exception, the Palestinian alumni deemed Oslo to have failed because it made the Palestinian situation worse and made the PA a tool of the occupation. They deemed the only beneficiary to be Fateh (the faction which runs the PA).

The exception to the general consensus was one alumnus who thought that Oslo brought the Palestinians a step nearer to self-determination and who claimed that 'the Israelis didn't gain anything'. On this last point, another alumnus volunteered:

> I think the Oslo process succeeded in highlighting the Israeli divisions and in convincing the Israelis that this is not a personal conflict with Arabs and that they are part of international struggles. This also applies to the Palestinians.

The most nuanced and ambivalent Olive Tree Palestinian response was:

> I don't know a lot about Oslo when it was signed and I don't know the position of the Palestinian leadership then. I don't know if there is anything better than Oslo. I don't know and I can't imagine the current situation without Oslo. It is very hard. Would there be any representation for Palestinians, a Palestinian passport, Palestinian ministries, etc?

This person then went on to ponder the apparent downsides, such as security coordination, and the expansion of Israeli settlements, and concluded: 'The problem is we are the weaker side in the conflict and no one is standing with us.' In the words of another Olive Tree alumnus:

> Yes, the Oslo process has failed. We can say today it's dead and probably all efforts to revive it will fail. The process failed because the Israeli side lacked the will to solve the conflict and preferred to continue with its settlement policies, confiscate more land and expand its settlements and continue its violence and war against the Palestinians in the West Bank and Gaza at the expense of peace. The process failed because of the lack of international will to reach a solution and to pressure both sides of the conflict to achieve

that. The Western powers aligned themselves, specifically Washington, to the Israeli destructive policies which gave Israel signs that it can continue with its policies without fearing to be held accountable.

Another was more scathing:

It failed because the Zionist greed for Palestine continues, and because the racist Zionists can't accept any presence except Jewish presence on the land of Palestine. The Zionists never wanted peace.

So much for those who think cross-conflict dialogue tempers hostility! A more measured assessment was:

Yes it failed, otherwise we would be living in peace not in apartheid, division, and institutional racism. It failed because it wasn't fully implemented. There was no supervision for its implementation or any consequences for not implementing it and there isn't any willingness to renegotiate it.

Generally speaking, the Olive Tree Palestinian alumni appeared unaware of or unimpressed by the few specific ways in which the Oslo process had produced some limited benefits, such as those the non-Olive Tree respondents identified. Further, they did not endorse the views of their Israeli counterparts that Oslo was a positive development in so far as it showed the Israelis had recognized the Palestinians as a people.

How Views on Oslo Evolved Among Dialogue Participants

In the beginning, in November 2013, the Israeli members of the 5th Cohort all said that Oslo *had not succeeded*, though one said that it was important in so far as it created hope and introduced the possibility of a two-state solution which had been absent before. He/she and others saw hope dashed by the 2nd Intifada and the Israeli response, for which Oslo was not directly to blame, but by which it was discredited.

By the finish, in July 2016, these respondents asserted that Oslo had simply *failed* or been overtaken by events. On balance, they were of the view that Oslo had in fact, been counterproductive, since it strengthened hardliners. In stark contrast to non-Olive Tree Israeli respondents to the survey in July 2016, the 5th

Cohort Israelis did not conclude that the creation of the Palestinian Authority and autonomy in parts of the West Bank was a plus for the Palestinians since, they asserted, these measures had enabled Israel to sustain the occupation.

The shift in views between the first and last surveys would seem to reflect the combination of the 2014 Gaza war, which disrupted the flow of the Olive Tree dialogue for months, and the collapse of the peace process initiated by US Secretary of State John Kerry (mentioned previously). Thus, events in the region and their effects on the Programme may account, at least in part, for the more sombre assessments in 2016.

In their initial responses, the Palestinians of the 5th Olive Tree Cohort had two alternative takes on Oslo. Thus, some thought that Oslo was a failure, with Palestinians the biggest losers, because it brought about all the most insidious features of the occupation. Others, however, thought that the Palestinian leadership did not handle Oslo well and/or: 'No one was ready and still [are] not, to take a step further towards a safer life for the sake of both nationalities'.

By the finish, in July 2016, these Palestinian respondents gave a much more measured critique of Oslo. One talked about the horrors of lawlessness that followed the second Intifada and Israeli roll-back of the PA powers and infrastructure. From that perspective, Oslo at least provided for the maintenance of law and order inside the Palestinian areas, which was restored in 2005. Yet the responses also showed a recognition that Oslo had complicated the situation and provided an infrastructure that enabled perpetuation of the occupation – making it manageable for the Israelis. 'It gave legitimacy to the colonial structure and the Israeli occupation'; and meant 'a lot of rights and lands were given up by the Palestinian politicians'.

Some Conclusions

With respect to international involvement in the Israeli-Palestinian conflict, it is clear from the assessments of both the Palestinians and the Israelis surveyed for this study that both parties see their conflict as part of a much wider contest of wills and objectives. Both identified the Europeans as major players in the genesis of the conflict, and Zionism as having been born in Europe in the context of European nationalist movements which magnified a long tradition of anti-Semitism in Europe.

The drive for Israeli statehood, a safe haven for Jews, as depicted by Israeli respondents, became an even more pressing imperative in the context of the

Holocaust. They saw the Arab states as hostile to their cause. Also, the Israeli respondents did not appear to see themselves as beholden to external support or as the fortunate winners in a contest between two nationalities. On the contrary, they conveyed a sense of having survived and thrived in the face of formidable odds and as being the best protectors of their own safety.

Portraying the Europeans as bearing prime responsibility for the emergence of Zionism, the Palestinians also saw the Europeans as the ones responsible for exporting Zionism into their midst. They attributed the strength of Israel and neglect of Palestinian rights to the support Israel received from external actors over time. They saw themselves as the enduring victims of *both* Israeli actions and the machinations of foreign powers.

In keeping with these contrasting depictions of their respective fates, in their assessments of the Oslo process, both parties judged it on the basis of what it meant for them. The Israelis deemed Oslo a turning point, in so far as it meant they had conceded the existence of another, rival, nationalist cause. The Palestinians also saw Oslo as a turning point, but as the introduction of mechanisms that had come to compound their inferior status.

To the Palestinians, Olive Tree and non-Olive Tree, the legacy of Oslo was to enable the continuation of the occupation of the West Bank, and blockade of the Gaza Strip, essentially by agreement between their leaders and the Israelis. Some blamed their leaders for naivety and incompetence. Others simply saw the process as flawed and inequitable from the start. Overall, the Palestinians conveyed the sense that they felt betrayed and misled. They did not, however, give much heed to the role of external actors in promoting Oslo and subsequent iterations of that formula. Instead, they lamented the concessions that their side had made to negative effect.

As discussed in the next Chapter, for the non-Olive Tree Palestinians, Oslo was a failure and a mistake, which had to be reversed. Yet, as will be seen, they wanted first to set their own house in order. For the Olive Tree Palestinians, however, there was greater awareness that the infrastructure of the occupation post Oslo was not the main issue. The key for them was to achieve recognition of their individual and national rights, on a par with, not inferior to, Israelis.

To the Israelis, particularly those in the 'comparator group', Oslo still represented a framework within which they could, ultimately, foresee negotiating a deal. It had, however, been overtaken by changes within both the Israeli and the Palestinian communities. Hardliners, against compromise, had gained ground in Israel – partly because the Oslo legacy had made it easier for the Israelis to manage the conflict, and partly because the Palestinians refused to be satisfied with the kind of compromise that Oslo envisaged and were in any case divided among themselves. For the Olive Tree Israelis, meanwhile, the positive aspect of Oslo was Israeli recognition of the Palestinians. The negative aspect was that it had enabled a reconfiguration of the occupation and thus reduced the incentives for the Israelis to change their overall position.

7
What Should Happen Now?

The last question I asked the respondents to the survey conducted for this study was: 'What should happen now?' The most striking difference between the respondents who had participated in the Olive Tree dialogue exercise and those who had not, was in their levels of understanding of the underlying drivers of the conflict. While the non-Olive Tree respondents offered a bewildering array of prescriptions with considerable assertiveness and conviction, the Olive Tree respondents were much more reflective and sophisticated in their identifications of the factors and issues underlying the conflict and were much less prescriptive.

Overall, the Israelis and Palestinians who had participated in three-years of cross-conflict dialogue, conducted in parallel with their undergraduate degree programmes in London, revealed a deep sense of concern about trends in their own society and that of their opponents. Between them they gave a portrayal of two communities on the verge of crisis and in need of healing. The message here is that cross-conflict dialogue, provided it is designed to be an exploratory, learning exercise rather than a problem solving one, and assuming it is facilitated in a supportive and non-judgemental way, enables deeper understanding.

In keeping with the findings of the work undertaken by William Perry and others following in his footsteps – discussed in Chapter 2 – the dialogue participants had clearly moved from a position of 'dualism', through 'relativism' to one of acceptance of diversity and complexity – though *not* acceptance of inequality on the basis of religion, culture or ethnicity. Accordingly, these participants were not inclined to endorse any of the oft-repeated formulae advocated by so many of the international actors who have tried their hand at conflict resolution in the Israeli-Palestinian case and discussed in Chapter 6. Instead, they ventured various ideas for transforming public perceptions and commonly held assumptions about self and other, with a view to helping both societies reappraise their circumstances in a new light and prioritise ending the asymmetries in their relations.

It is much harder to approach reality in this vein than to hold onto dualistic notions about right and wrong, what 'we' need and what 'they' will have to come to terms with. No surprise, therefore, that policymakers prefer mechanistic prescriptions for dividing up the pie between the parties and ignoring the narrative issues. If this work has been about anything, it has demonstrated that there can be no side-lining or parking of the national narratives – because these are the drivers and the life blood of the conflict. Yet coming to terms with this reality demands bravery, standing back from the fray and withstanding the insults of those who prefer simplistic analyses and quick fixes. No wonder then that so many of the Olive Tree respondents to the survey professed themselves unsure as to how to proceed. The good news, however, is that they accepted this state of uncertainty as preferable to denial.

To illustrate this point further, the non-Olive Tree respondents to the survey stated their views with confidence and came up with all sorts of proposals for fixing the situation which were logical in terms of their own needs, but which required others to change more than them. In so doing, these non-Olive Tree respondents did not however, reveal much if any consensus among themselves on 'what next?' As the would-be peacemakers have discovered, moving forward is not possible without consensus on the path to be taken.[1] Both Israelis and Palestinians are divided among themselves on what best to do now, which opens the way for political leaders to play to the lowest common denominator and keep repeating their desire for an end to conflict, while allowing inertia to take its course.

In what follows I have quoted at length the survey responses of the Olive Tree and non-Olive Tree respondents to the question 'What should happen now?' the better to enable the reader to judge the veracity of the assessments offered in this introduction.

Israeli Thoughts on 'What should happen now?'

It will be recalled that when Israeli survey respondents were asked about what the Palestinians want now (see Chapter 5), all the Olive Tree alumni correctly identified what their Palestinian counterparts themselves said they wanted – freedom, rights, an end to occupation. By contrast, the 'comparator group', non-Olive Tree Israeli respondents, simply speculated on how much land and sovereignty the Palestinians aspired to obtain and what they might settle for. There were several echoes of these distinctions in the Olive Tree and non-Olive

---

[1] As explored, in respect to Israel, in Heller, M. and Rosemary Hollis, eds. (2005) *Israel and the Palestinians: Israeli Policy Options* Royal Institute of International Affairs.

Tree Israeli responses to the question: 'What should happen now?'

Non-Olive Tree Israeli Responses

All eight non-Olive Tree Israelis surveyed outlined a way forward toward peace, but their proposals varied enormously, from a revival of the Oslo process, to its abandonment, from a top down leadership approach to a bottom-up grass-roots approach, and from a two-state solution to a one-state binational formula. One wanted change in both the Israeli and Palestinian leaderships, as a prelude to peace-making, another saw a change in the Palestinian leadership as essential. Here are two examples of the more assertive responses:

1. Two states for two people, based on mutual agreement, not on unilateral moves. In addition, certain areas of the [West] Bank, which can be strengthened economically and socially, should be identified and mechanisms that will allow cooperation with the Israeli economy and society ('social-economic peace') should be established. Furthermore, an alternative to the current Palestinian leadership, that could stand strong in the face of the strengthening political and radical Islam, should be built [i.e. *established – translator's note*]. This leadership should be supported with the ability to mobilise in the territory and the nurturing of the next generation.

2. Both sides should sit down for negotiations and agree on the principles which will bring the conflict to an end. There are dozens of plans aiming to bring the conflict to an end out there (the Roadmap, Clinton Parameters, the Geneva Initiative and more) – what is needed now is for the leaders of both sides to exhibit courage and willingness in order to reach substantial compromises and present their people with a plan which will enable both sides to have a better future. Today there are some regional initiatives (the initiative of the Egyptian President Sisi, 'the Arab Peace Initiative') and international initiatives (the French initiative, the Quartet report which was published this month [July 2016] and a possible UN Security Council resolution after the US elections or during the final months of Obama's presidency) aimed at supporting both sides and providing Israel with security guarantees. Obviously, this evaluation represents what I think *should* happen and

160

not what I think will happen in practice.

And here are two of the more reflective responses of non-Olive Tree Israelis:

1. Since the idea of two states is inapplicable [*as in not feasible, perhaps, but not clear*] and does not solve the main, fundamental problems, we should look for solutions elsewhere and try a few different modes of action. The first thing that must be changed, if we wish to ignite a deep and fundamental process, is the educational aspect. Today it may seem unrealistic and inapplicable, but until both sides are educated toward recognition and understanding of the other's narrative, without necessarily accepting it or agreeing with it, true progress cannot be made. In a situation in which each side is certain of its own righteousness and legitimacy while the other side is being disregarded, this simply cannot happen. On the theoretical level, we must think of applicable solutions, different to the two-state solution. The spectrum of frameworks available, from a confederation to two-states in one space, can become the foundation for finding the right framework. The solution will not be perfect, but there are a few directions with the potential to sooth the conflict better than the rickety and artificial separation offered by the two states notion. That way, there will be no need to evacuate settlements, as the situation today is that both people are so mixed outside of the Green Line that it is too late to separate them. This is no less of an illusion than to think it is possible to bring about such a separation. What restricts the conflict today is the intellectual stagnation and the perpetual return to the Oslo paradigm. Only when other directions, as wild as they may seem, will be examined in depth will we be able to truly deal with the difficult questions at hand and understand how they can be dealt with. This way or another, these are long and complex processes, which require patience. Considering the Israeli and Palestinian reality today, there is not much space for optimism.

2. Today, the different publics should choose how they want to view the future of Eretz Israel and elect the political leaders who will bring them there. As long as the Israeli public believes that the current situation is the best option for them, and that it is in line with the values

of a Jewish-democratic state, the Israeli leadership will continue acting towards the preservation of the situation. The Palestinian public, for its part, will soon stand a civilian test once Abbas steps down from the Palestinian leadership. The Palestinians will then have to decide whether they are coming together to determine who their leaders will be and in which direction will the Palestinian national ship be navigated.

Israeli Olive Tree Alumni Responses

Of the ten Olive Tree Israeli alumni respondents to the survey (excluding those of the 5th Cohort – on which more below), only one called for the two-state solution and in doing so prioritised creation of a Palestinian state, thus:

1.   A Palestinian state should be established in the territories of Judea and Samaria. The big settlement blocs should be annexed to Israel, with the possibility of territorial exchanges in order to compensate the Palestinians. This will prevent, as much as possible, the evacuation of settlers. The Palestinian leaders should announce the abandonment of the armed struggle and lay down their arms. The Palestinian state should be, at the initial stage, demilitarised. The refugees could repatriate to the territory of the newly established Palestinian state and receive compensation. The holy sites in Jerusalem could reside under either shared or international sovereignty. If Hamas agrees to disarm, it too can take a part in the process.

Three Israeli alumni could not identify a way forward. Their responses were:

2.   Unfortunately, in the current political climate it is very difficult to imagine that there is even a next step to be taken. Two states probably won't happen because the settlements are receiving more and more funding from the government. One nation state will not be established because it will turn the state into a 'state of all its citizens' instead of a state in which the white Jews rule and all the others obey.

3.   I don't know. We are at a disheartening political low point. The international struggle against the Israeli state, over the occupation and its

162

discriminatory rule (apartheid), should be enhanced.

4. It is difficult to say. It seems that the steps necessary for peace are not realistic – replacing the leaders and reducing the hatred seem like impossible tasks. However, smaller steps such as private reconciliation initiatives (like the Olive Tree) and international pressure over the government [*could*] help realise the processes necessary for beginning peace talks.

Two respondents called for more international pressure on the Israeli government to oblige it to be more open to compromise, but they and others also advocated more international support for Israeli civil society and one of these said pressure groups such as the Boycott, Divestment and Sanctions (BDS) movement were counter-productive.

Six of the ten respondents called for a fundamental rethink of the conflict, new ideas and societal change on both sides. Here are three examples:

a) Working on the field level (grassroots), and any higher level possible, towards the maturity and preparation of the communities for what is necessary to be done in order to progress on the educational, economic and discourse levels.

b) In my opinion it will take at least one more generation, if not longer, until the approaches of both sides will change and the peoples [*nations – translator's note*] will understand that there is no purpose in a never-ending conflict, as happened in Europe after hundreds of years of conflict.

c) ....it is important to note, that, in my opinion, there is currently no politically fertile ground for talks. The Israeli coalitionary makeup must change in order to progress in this area. On the other hand, there is the fear that the moderate voices in the Palestinian Authority will continue to weaken. The design of peace talks must deal with the issue of identities, with security as a component of the one [*Israeli*] identity and with the refugees and the right of return as components of the other [*Palestinian*] identity – and discuss these issues using tools which allow inclusion. Openness for other solutions – in view of the current political climate – is necessary, to consider new ideas, beyond the two-state solution. For example, a federation of two states (an Israel with a Palestinian minority and a Palestine with a Jewish/Israeli minority, Jerusalem as a joint capital, joint federal institutions with national institutions remaining on the individual state level). This format has the potential to bridge between the different identities and allow them to exist in parallel and cooperate while still realising the national self-determination of both people.

Overall, the alumni proposals for what should happen now manifested awareness of the identity and narrative issues discussed in Olive Tree. Also, the Olive Tree alumni were somewhat more critical of their own side than the non-Olive Tree Israelis, and more cognisant of the Palestinian reality, their needs and aspirations. Interestingly, none of them advocated a return to the peace process as previously pursued in the 1990s and early 2000s. They also did not talk about territorial compromises, with the exception of the first and last ones quoted.

The effect of the Olive Tree dialogue, over three years, was, I contend, to render the Israeli participants much more aware of the complexities of the conflict, the role of incompatible national narratives and the value of attitudinal changes to make resolution possible. One, quoted above, actually volunteered that more Olive Tree type initiatives would be helpful.

The Longitudinal Study: Israelis

In November 2013 one Israeli respondent volunteered no response at all to the question 'What should happen now?', while another said he/she wanted more international intervention to resolve the conflict. By 2016 both these Israelis gave responses that identified the most pressing problem as increasingly acrimonious divisions within Israeli society. Both wanted efforts to be focused on tackling racism and reversing Israeli denial of the Palestinians and their narrative as a route to retrieving the legitimacy and ideals they wanted Israel to embody. Their argument spoke of a desire to, as it were, 'do unto the Palestinians what they would have done unto themselves'.

Another Israeli respondent said in 2013 that he/she wanted a two-state solution to the conflict to be achieved by gradual steps and the creation of a positive dynamic. In 2016 this respondent again articulated the necessity of reaching a solution by gradual steps, providing considerably more detail on what this would entail, including a significant improvement in the daily lives of the Palestinians; an end to the siege of Gaza, and a decision by Hamas to accept Israel and cease resistance. She/he also proposed an end to 'the settlement enterprise' in the West Bank and Palestinian sovereignty over the whole of the West Bank, whether as part of a two-state agreement or not.

The fourth Israeli respondent offered an idiosyncratic proposal in 2013 which would involve no right of return for Palestinians and no return of Jews to their places of origin in Europe, Africa, Iraq and Iran. She/he also opposed automatic citizenship of Israel for Jews around the world and called for an end to settlement building; the punishment of soldiers who flout international law, and the building of economic relations between Israelis and Palestinians. He/she said: 'There will be two countries that use the same money and have free entrance for all – like in Europe.' He/she did not revisit these propositions in 2016, but instead called for international pressure to bring about compromise between the parties. Absent this, she/he warned, more war was inevitable and would bring its own transformation and changes of perception.

In summary, there was a shift in all the positions of the respondents, reflecting rising concerns and fears about the trends they observed. All called for change, especially in Israeli thinking about the situation.

Palestinian Thoughts on 'What should happen now?'
Looking first at the survey responses of the non-Olive Tree Palestinians, it will be remembered, as explained in Chapter 2 and repeated periodically thereafter, that these respondents answered all the survey questions in a 'focus group'. On the issue of 'What should happen now?' as with the earlier questions about Oslo (discussed in Chapter 6) the group became animated. Many saw a need to put their own house in order before proceeding to a new stage in their conflict with the Israelis.

Non-Olive Tree Palestinian Responses
The consensus among the respondents was that Oslo needed to be revoked and the PA fundamentally reformed or dismantled. They debated what to replace it with, but had fewer concerns about that than with the need for 'change from within', full representation, Palestinian unity – both at the leadership level (end-

ing Fateh and Hamas divisions) and geographically (between the West Bank and Gaza). They called for an end to corruption, an end to 'old guard' leadership and for its replacement with 'the new generation' and a 'new ideology'. For all of them these were the priorities before considering what to do about the Israelis and/or considering peace options or possibilities.

Here are some examples of what they said:

- There must be change.
- We need to revoke the Oslo agreement.
- When I was a child, children used to tell their fathers 'I want to become a doctor or an engineer'. I used to tell my father 'I want to join the army when I grow up'. When I grew up, I discovered we didn't have an army. Tomorrow we will have an army and a government like all other countries. I don't want partial independence. Arab countries are partially independent. The Syrian Golan, for example, is still occupied by Israel. Sinai is controlled by Israel. We want full rule and full sovereignty.
- We can learn from the Algerian Revolution. When it gained independence from the French occupation they didn't have a government. The people elected a government, and I think Ahmad Ben Bella became the first president. Why can't we learn from the Algerian revolution? There were problems and the people fought each other but that would still be better than the occupation's crimes against us. After that the people managed to create a system and order. Liberation is not easy. Liberation needs a lot of work.
- In my opinion changing the occupation comes from within us. We need to change ourselves and then we can change the reality of the occupation. In my opinion every revolution has a leader.....The leader speaks in the name of the people because all the people support him.... not fake elections and no corruption. There is a lot of corruption here. The people have lost trust.
- For me ending the division between the West Bank and Gaza Strip and having unity between the West Bank and Gaza Strip are most important. After that we can think of changing things for the better.
- Ending the division is the first step. We need national unity and if this doesn't work then the PA should be dissolved. We don't want the PA.

This way we will be under civil administration[2] and under one government rather than under both the PA and Israel. We can coexist with them [*Israelis*] if this is the only solution. We used to travel freely and the situation was better. We should go back to the civil administration.

- I say in the current period we need to end corruption. They need to hand over the legislative council to educated people. We shouldn't be buying votes with calling credit. We shouldn't create corruption to make sure we are elected. We need to end corruption and then we can talk about the occupation.

- The people, especially the younger generation, are more aware. There are leaders that have better understanding of the situation. They are not hypocrites like the leaders of the first intifada. They are not afraid of telling the truth. They can have an aware and rational discussion with their parents. I can see that in 4 or maximum 7 years we need to dissolve the PA and then immediately end the occupation.

- The most important thing is ending the occupation and gaining independence. No more checkpoints. I think internally Palestinian reconciliation is the most important thing. After that ending the corruption in the institutions and creating jobs for graduates and Palestinian workers who wait 2 or 3 hours every day at checkpoints to enter Israel to earn a living. Some of these workers are even killed on the checkpoints. Those are the most important things.

- There should be elections because the people are tired of the same faces. We need new ideology; the new generation is more aware and educated. It shouldn't be just old people. There are young people who are intellectuals. After that there are a lot of people who are living in ignorance. They don't know anything about their cause, politics or culture. If you ask them questions about politics they say I'm not interested. Everyone should be interested in politics. There should be a political revolution from the people.

As is clear from all of the above, the mood among the Palestinians in the 'focus group' in Ramallah in July 2016 was essentially in favour of a compre-

---

[2] Before the creation of the PA Israel staffed and ran a department of 'civil administration' in the West Bank and Gaza.

hensive revolution in their own community and then a return to conflict (or negotiations). So preoccupied with this imperative were they that they said next to nothing about what relationship they wanted with the Israelis down the line. An end to occupation and Palestinian sovereignty, but under a totally new and younger leadership, was their goal.

Palestinian Olive Tree Alumni Responses

The Palestinian Olive Tree alumni did not call for a revolution against the PA, though they did not defend the PA either. Their focus was on the need to end the occupation and they assumed that since the Palestinians are too weak to bring this about by themselves, it would have to come as a result of international action. These respondents also identified mounting internal pressures for more intense conflict, but, unlike their non-Olive Tree counterparts, they did not seek to bring it on.

Here are some examples of what they said should happen now:

- I think equating between the Israelis and the Palestinians is not fair. There is a ruler and ruled; a colonialist and colonized. The Israeli side needs to take the initiative to end the occupation and the colonization. The ball is in their court. There needs to be international economic and political pressure on Israel to end the occupation. Alternatives need to be found. Of course, this is not possible because Israel is not interested in peace.

- The situation on the ground is very hard and complicated and doesn't show any signs that a solution to the conflict can be reached. The chances for peace are quickly disappearing. Unless the international community intervenes and pressures Israel to stop its settlement policies and violence against the Palestinians it would be very hard to talk about any prospect for peace. Unless the Palestinians are active internally and internationally their cause will be marginalized or forgotten, as the world would be busy with wars and bigger crises in the region.

- Bring peace to the region and allow the refugees to return.

- Stop the killing; stop the oppression; peace.

- Palestinians should be given their rights as soon as possible; Palestinian suffering should end; Palestinians should feel free and secure; Palestinians should be allowed to return to the homes they were forced to leave; Palestinians should be compensated for all they have suffered at the hands of European colonialists and the Zionists.

- I think Palestinian entrepreneurs, businessmen, and agents should start up infrastructure initiatives and keep pushing to achieve such initiatives and projects such as clean water, energy, fast internet, sewage treatment, IT/Software projects, and many other similar projects that benefit communities and make the Palestinians ready to have a state. I believe this will be the key for obtaining a Palestinian state.
- I have no clue and, sometimes, I do not even care. I am really sick of the whole situation. For us Palestinians, I believe, we need to work and build our future; educate our children; further invest in the youth; promote human rights, gender-equality and social justice and enhance our economy despite the Israeli occupation. We have to live with the occupation but also improve our situation and face the many social ills in our society caused sometimes by backwardness or religion or both, although both are highly correlated, I think.
- A third party should control everything on the ground in the Palestinian and Israeli life and to treat the two sides like one people. The country that doesn't have any historic relations or religious advantage is China.

The following Olive Tree response bore the most resemblance to the thinking among non-Olive Tree Palestinians:

The solution for me is that the PA should dissolve itself. We should be on paper like we are in reality: under occupation. Israel should assume the costs of the current situation. Making the occupation costly might change this horrible situation. Negotiations will not help. We tried negotiations for 68 years and they didn't change anything. We need to try something new. The PA for me is part of the problem and should go. Israel is not losing much with the continuation of the occupation. That's why we need to make it very costly; maybe this will lead to a change

Clearly, there can be no avoiding the conclusion that for the Olive Tree Palestinian alumni the occupation was their overriding concern. That also came out in their responses to the question: 'What do the Palestinians want now?'

discussed in Chapter 5. The message here, I believe, is that the focus of would-be peacemakers needs to be on ending the occupation and the exact modality of achieving that is less important than simply bringing it to an end. I also detect here some sense of agency about making life in the Palestinian community better, provided that is, that an end to the occupation is also envisaged.

The Longitudinal Study: Palestinians

In their initial responses, in November 2013, the 5th Cohort Palestinians called for equal rights and an end to Israeli dominance, irrespective of whether that be achieved through two states or one. Some also called for more opportunities for dialogue between ordinary people, and more initiatives like the Olive Tree scholarships.

Here are a couple of illustrations:

- The best solution that I can think of and the fairest one to everybody is one Palestinian state, that grants the current Jewish residents of the land the right to live in the land they call home, while stopping the overwhelming immigration of the so-called 'Jews' to Palestine, where there will be a secular state with equal rights for all its Palestinians regardless of their religious beliefs and spiritual practices.
- I genuinely believe that there is a place for everybody in the 'holy land'. And it's not 'victory' that I seek or demand, rather it's justice. How to achieve that is a complicated question that not only Palestinians should attempt to answer, but all those who are interested in peace, democracy and social justice around the world.

By the finish, in July 2016, the Palestinian responses echoed those of the Israelis who identified a crisis in Israeli society and speculated that this could in itself turn into an agent of change. They were clear, in any case, that the need was for an end to deprivation and the dawn of equality. Interestingly though, while the Israeli respondents were most conscious of the potential for civil strife in Israel, the Palestinians voiced a sense of foreboding about the likelihood of an explosion of the situation in the West Bank.

Here are three examples:

1. I don't know if I have any answer for this question. I think because of the deteriorating political situation and the absence of the international community's support for a radical change, Israel will or could suffer a great loss that would make it stop its aggression and stop violating international laws and duties. All the Palestinians want is to have an effective long-term peace deal that guarantees them living in peace.

2. Peace. Nothing. I don't know. Like I control what should happen now! Any ideal answer would be around the principle of peace and giving people their rights because they are people not because they are Palestinians, Israelis, Jews or Arabs. Stop the killing. Stop the massacres. Massacres will lead only to more problems and more wars and nothing more. But this will not happen. What will happen is what always happens. Anything that will happen will be in the interests of the stronger side. The weaker side is the Palestinian side not the Israeli one. I don't know for how long this will continue to be in the interest of the stronger party. But it must end. For sure it will end; but when and how? This is a very complicated process and I'm afraid that blood and killing could be part of it. I don't want to think about it. I doubt my humanity when I think of the bloodshed and killing of innocents. The weak Palestinian leadership tries to get some rights or gain more control through fighting the enemy with diplomacy, but it's hard. The media has brainwashed many people about the Palestinian cause. It's a very hard thing to do and needs a lot of patience and sacrifice. Israel is not interested in peace or to be more accurate is interested in peace that serves its interests and increases the burdens in our life, future, history and our land. Honestly, I can't think of one answer for this question. I don't want to talk about myths like the 1967 borders and so on because they are media illusions or decisions that are not valuable on the ground and will never be implemented. I'm not a pessimist but I feel this is the truth because I feel something needs to happen to change things and restore rights. People who have rights are people and I mean that there shouldn't be anyone oppressed in the land called Palestine.

3. I think the struggle in the region needs civil wars for it to be solved. I think the success of Iran, Saudi Arabia, Turkey and Egypt in maintaining the state structures makes Israel the weaker link. It is full of

ethnic conflicts and political failures. The divisions on the ground and the state of poverty that led to increasing settlements have intensified internal Israeli struggle. Israel's repeated failure in finding military solutions for its regional conflicts makes it under siege psychologically, socially and culturally. Israel is not necessarily the problem but rather the social, economic and political conflict in the region. We are on the verge of a civil war in the West Bank. The settlers will create a situation where the Israeli army has to either stand with the settlers against the Palestinians and to expel them from their land and take over the land or between a regional situation where the Israeli army fails to withstand such a state for a long period of time. Israel is facing many conflicts and the Israeli army is surrounded internally and externally. The Palestinians are contributing their blood which is the only thing they can do to stay on their land and to intensify the Israeli failure. I think Abbas's death will spark a civil war in which Israel would lose the battle on the ground and lose the diplomatic battle. The Israeli army won't be able to defend the land and the people at the same time. The Israelis won't be able to live in the cities in safety for a long time if such a war starts.

Some Conclusions

The main conclusions of this whole study are identified in the next and final chapter, so for now I offer only some concluding thoughts on the material presented in this chapter. What stands out here is the contrast between the journey taken by Israeli participants in the Olive Tree Programme and that taken by the Palestinians.

The Israelis learned that the creation of a Palestinian Authority (under the Oslo process) did not give the Palestinians something approaching collective equality with the Israeli collective entity. It did not prove a step toward a two-state solution. Rather, it placed the Palestinians under two levels of control, one local (the PA) and one national (Israel). In terms of the evolution of thinking in Israeli society over the decades, the Olive Tree Israelis did see Oslo as a plus, in so far as it marked Israeli recognition of the Palestinians as a separate national community desirous of its own government – yet in terms of the implementation of Oslo, Israel remained in overall control and the PA proved more of a mechanism for maintaining the occupation than one for ending it. And the

Israelis learned that the Palestinians hate being under occupation and want it to end.

The Israelis also learned that they could not convince their Palestinian counterparts in Olive Tree that their own side felt obliged to continue the occupation until the Palestinians could convince them that they would not constitute a threat to Israel if only the occupation was ended. Instead, they came to see that by their actions, in particular the expansion of settlements, blockade of the Gaza Strip and periodic resorts to war on that front, the Israeli government and a significant body of Israeli opinion, did not want to do what it would take, on their part, to make way for a truly independent Palestinian national entity. Thus, the Olive Tree Israelis came to identify the obstacles to peace as lying as much within their own society as having to do with faults and flaws in Palestinian thinking and behaviour. Many of them concluded that they could not justify the official positions of their own side and were saddened by the betrayal of the values that they had understood their country to stand for.

The Palestinian participants in Olive Tree learned that, on a one-to-one basis they lacked most of the freedoms and opportunities which their Israeli counterparts took for granted. Many of them actually quite liked the Israeli individuals they came to know personally through the Olive Tree and could find common ground with them as fellow university students in London and, indeed, as individuals who knew so much more about their part of the world, their history and the peculiarities of their conflict than any of those other students at the university. What the Olive Tree Palestinians could and would not do, however, for the duration of the Programme, was accept the official Israeli narrative, whether espoused by their Israeli colleagues or not, as excusing their collective situation back home. They listened to and learned from the Israeli explanations for the official Israeli narrative, but made it their business to persuade their Israeli counterparts that this narrative *and* Israeli fears for their safety could not justify the plight of the Palestinians.

When war broke out on the Gaza front, as it did on at least one occasion during the time spent in London by each of the Olive Tree Cohorts, and when violence erupted in East Jerusalem and the West Bank, both the Israeli and the Palestinian participants identified with their respective societies back home, not with each other. That said, many Israeli individuals in the Programme did try to reach out to their Palestinian counterparts suffering anxiety about the safety of their relatives and friends. The Palestinians acknowledged these gestures and made it clear they did not hold their Israeli colleagues personally responsible. Yet they also did not portray the decisions of their own leaders, of whom they could be highly critical at times, as on a par with the decisions of the Israeli leaders.

In sum, the asymmetries in the conflict were reflected in the Olive Tree dialogue. The learnings of the Israeli and Palestinian participants were very different, both about themselves and the other. Yet both came out with an even stronger desire to see the conflict resolved than they started with; both identified the need for a change in how Israelis in general understand the Palestinians; and both wanted the Palestinians to be free.

Conclusions

The main conclusion of this work is that we need to take much more seriously than we generally do the role of group or national narratives as drivers of conflict. These narratives are binary constructs, that tell us who we are and who we are not and, as a result, can incline us to demonise and dehumanise the 'other' or enemy. What we think is *the* truth is often only our version of it and so attached are we to *our* storyline that we will stick with it even in the face of contradictory evidence.

Group narratives are defined here as stories or explications that draw on collective memories, historical experiences, seminal texts and myths from which may be derived meanings and values, and which define the group. They identify our heroes and role models, as well as our demons and enemies. They tell us what makes us good and our actions rational, and others less good and irrational. They make sense of our emotional reactions to the situations we find ourselves in and to those whom we have learned to fear. Yet they are not pure inventions. On the contrary, they make reference to real occurrences or 'facts,' but do so selectively and subjectively. They are underpinned by the prevailing balance (or imbalance) of power in our relations with others.

Our national narratives function like stories, with the plot lines and character roles already sketched out for us when we are born. They become drivers or imperatives to act, and react, to others, in accordance with the internal logic of the story, rather than on the basis of non-partisan or detached analysis. As such they explain why the actors in a conflict may refuse to compromise, even when that means losing opportunities to make peace, because these actors feel compelled by circumstance, or duty-bound, to conform to the roles assigned by their group identity.

It is in this sense that the actors in a conflict can become trapped by their narratives into endless rounds of hostilities, unable to detach themselves sufficiently to review their situation or story objectively or separate from it. Yet to argue that someone *ought* to be able to separate from their narrative is akin to arguing that they should give up their identity – which, in a conflict, is hardly in their power. Individual choices are limited when exclusivist group narratives dominate. The reality or norm is thus the coexistence of several competing narratives operating in parallel.

The Research Framework

This depiction of national narratives as binary constructs and thence conflict drivers is based on the findings of a multi-year research project that I was able to undertake as a result of becoming the director of the Olive Tree Programme for Israelis and Palestinians awarded scholarships to study for undergraduate degrees at City, University of London, between 2008 and 2016. The details of that endeavour are provided in Chapter 2 and referenced throughout this book, and while the resulting discoveries relate to the ongoing conflict between Palestinians and Israelis, the lessons to be drawn have relevance in other settings and disputes where identity issues are at stake.

The realisation that competing national narratives operate in parallel with one another in a conflict came about during the course of the cross-conflict dialogue that formed part of the Olive Tree Programme. This revelation was not anticipated in advance or an intended outcome. Instead, the significance of the narratives as part and parcel of the Israeli-Palestinian conflict became manifest during interactions between the Israelis and Palestinians participating in the Programme, as explained previously and recapped below.

Further discoveries were made as the result of the survey exercise I decided to undertake, between 2013 and 2016. For the details of this, including the questions asked, again I refer the reader to Chapter 2. It identified the main components of the Palestinian and Israeli national narratives, including the ways in which they each depict 'self' and 'other' in a binary combination. It also revealed which elements of the narratives are so internalized as to be considered fundamental and beyond dispute, and which are amenable to reconsideration under certain circumstances.

As summarised below, the elements in the Israeli narrative about which doubts can surface in the minds of at least some Israelis are: the foundations of Palestinian national identity and rights; the motivations and aspirations of the Palestinians today; and the morality of maintaining the occupation. The elements in the Palestinian narrative which can become open to question among Palestinians, given the opportunity, are: the range of roles available to them as defenders of the national cause; the contemporary drivers of the conflict; and the commonly assumed equation between 'talking to the enemy' and 'normalisation'.

Parallel Narratives

The protagonists in the Israeli-Palestinian conflict understand the main episodes or milestones in the history of that conflict in fundamentally different ways. This was revealed during the dialogue in which successive cohorts of Israeli and Palestinian scholarship students participated while studying for their undergraduate degrees at City. What follows is a recap of how this discovery came about.

The practice I adopted with each cohort of students, during my time as director of Olive Tree, was to begin by exposing them to the views of various experts, including politicians and academics espousing different perspectives. After several weeks of this, the students became impatient. Almost all of them found something to question or disagree with in what they heard. They wanted to explore for themselves.

Consequently, my co-facilitator and I decided to invite the students to start exploring some aspects of their own upbringing and acculturation. We invited them to identify and compare the fairy tales and stories they had been told as children and how these depicted heroes and villains, and how they were enjoined to emulate the former and fear the latter. They reflected on the ways in which stories had taught them values and what was expected of them in terms of serving their communities and national cause.

Then we asked them to identify iconic images that held an enduring significance and message for them. Almost all of these turned out to feature some aspect or episode in the conflict – for example, the wreckage of a bus blown up, along with its passengers, in a suicide bomb attack; a confrontation between armed soldiers and unarmed demonstrators; a refugee camp juxtaposed with a hilltop settlement; an injured and bloodied child screaming.

This latter exercise drew everyone into discussion of the conflict, and it was at this point that it was decided that the students would pick out one or other of the key episodes or turning points in the conflict for investigation. These included the wars of 1948, 1967 and 1973, the first and second Intifadas. In their respective national groups, the students then researched how their mainstream national narrative recorded and explained the event in question. They were requested *not* to give their personal opinions, but rather to compile a presentation – drawing on conversations with relatives and friends, examination of the textbooks they had used at school, internet sources, etc. – on how that episode was portrayed in their narrative.

What emerged were contrasting depictions of what had occurred and the significance of that – for one side or both. The effect was salutary. Each of the presentations conveyed the power of the respective narratives to recount the same moment in history in palpably different ways. Their strength and appeal lies in their story-like format, featuring heroic deeds and charismatic characters.

By comparing the explanatory power of two or more such narratives, it became clear that each narrative makes sense in isolation and follows its own internal logic. They exist in parallel and only partially intersect. They defy amalgamation or reconciliation. The comparison also showed that facts are not understood objectively, but in terms of the implications for one side or the other.

The conclusion drawn was that the conflict cannot be understood except as a combination of competing narratives *and* facts. Also, since the narratives distinguish between 'us' and 'them', they tend to blame the 'other' for forcing each group to behave in the ways they do. They militate against befriending 'the other' because that would be to betray one's identity, as enshrined in the narrative.

Constants and Variables in the Narratives

Now I turn to some of the lessons to be drawn from the survey exercise undertaken specifically for this study. As noted above, the details of that survey are explained in Chapter 2. In essence, it was designed to establish the main tenets of the Israeli and Palestinian national narratives as internalised by some of the protagonists, where they converge, and where they diverge or contrast most prominently.

It was also intended to explore how and to what extent new knowledge and insights, gleaned through first-hand interaction with the opposite side, might change how the protagonists describe themselves and the other, or otherwise recalibrate their narratives. Put differently, it served to indicate which components of the Palestinian and Israeli national narratives are fundamental and beyond question for these nationalities and which are amenable to questioning or revision.

It is important to note here that the survey was not a public opinion poll and did *not* include a cross-section of both societies. Rather, the main respondents were alumni of the Olive Tree Programme and, as such, relatively well-educated, aspiring professionals and broadly secular. The kind of people who might be expected to aspire to political (but not religious) leadership positions in their respective societies. They came from across Israel, the Gaza Strip and the West

178

Bank. They had all had the experience of living in London, gaining degrees and engaging in dialogue with each other. They were therefore comparable with each other in many respects.

To add another dimension to the survey, two 'comparator' groups, one Israeli and one Palestinian, were also asked to participate in the survey. They were of the same age range (their 20s and 30s) as the Olive Tree respondents, mostly graduates of or students at local universities, and comparable to the Olive Tree alumni in that sense, but unlike them in that they had not been exposed to intensive cross-conflict dialogue. The responses were given anonymously and in either Hebrew or Arabic.

Self and Other

Chapter 3 explored how the Israeli and Palestinian respondents defined themselves and the other. In broad summary: The Israelis defined themselves in a way that ascribed central importance to the state and the obligations of citizenship of that state. They all identified Jewishness, Zionism and 'living in fear' as attributes of 'Israeliness'. The Palestinians defined themselves as a people without a state, as exiles and refugees, and under occupation. They identified themselves as the original inhabitants and true owners of the land taken over by the Israelis.

Herein lies a stark contrast: these conflict protagonists primarily describe themselves in terms of either having a state or being deprived of one. They are trapped in inequality and their identities are derivative of that.

When asked to define Palestinians, Israeli respondents, especially those from the 'comparator' group, depicted them as envious and threatening, with aspirations which could endanger Jewish Israelis and their state. The comparator group respondents also denigrated the Palestinian national cause as a copycat response to Zionism. However, the Olive Tree Israelis did concede the legitimacy of Palestinian nationalism, framing it as a response to the occupation.

The Palestinians defined the Israelis as wanting to perpetuate the occupation and to deny Palestinian rights, while at the same time wanting an end to conflict and peace on their terms. They depicted the Israelis as the people who came from outside and took Palestinian land because of discrimination against them, but who now 'discriminate against us.'

Thus, while the Palestinians refuted the legitimacy of the Israeli state because it was built by outsiders and at their expense; the Israelis did not doubt the legitimacy of their state but differed on the legitimacy of the Palestinian national cause.

One of the messages here is that, according to this specific survey, the Israeli narrative celebrates the achievement of founding a state against opposition in 1948 and in that respect claims greater legitimacy for Israeli nationality. Those Israelis who do, or have come to, recognize Palestinian national identity, do so more on the basis of the occupation of 1967, than what happened in 1948. Palestinians refute Israeli national rights on the basis of their own loss in 1948 *and* the occupation. Both claims rely on different readings of history and militate against seeing 'the other' as equal or 'like us'.

National Narratives

As examined in Chapter 4, the mainstream (secular) Israeli national story is about state-building and the Palestinian national story is about expulsion, exile and refugee-ness.

Israeli respondents to the survey described their quest to create and consolidate a state as a necessity (given the persecution of the Jews in Europe) and a success, to which the Palestinians reacted with resistance. The Palestinians described themselves as the ones who lost out in the face of the Israeli state-building enterprise. In this sense, the two stories or histories are co-dependent but with opposite outcomes. The Palestinians saw their fate as the consequence of Israeli success, but the Israelis embraced their success as the result of their own efforts, notwithstanding Palestinian and other Arab opposition.

When asked to identify the origins of the conflict, Israeli survey respondents stated that the conflict began with Arab resistance to Jewish immigration and the foundation of Israel. Whereas the non-Olive Tree Israeli respondents saw this resistance as reactive and disorganised rather than a national struggle, Olive Tree Israelis explained the conflict as a clash between two national movements.

Several of the non-Olive Tree Palestinian survey respondents saw the Oslo Accords (1993 and '95) as the start of the contemporary conflict, neglecting to mention its origins before that. This demonstrated their preoccupation with living under occupation and the role of the Palestinian Authority in policing that occupation, as they saw it. When prompted, however, they attributed the origins of the conflict to the machinations of the imperial powers who carved up the region into separate states after World War I, and/or to the Holocaust, or, in some cases, to religion.

By contrast, Olive Tree Palestinians did not talk about imperialist plots or Western conspiracies, choosing instead to attribute the origins of the conflict to cycles of violence and retribution, Israeli settlement expansion and the occupation.

The message here is that, while not relinquishing their understanding of the legitimacy of the Israeli state, it is possible for Israelis to see the Palestinian national cause as real and in competition with their own. Yet, in coming to this view, such Israelis indicated a greater sense of insecurity. I would also note that those Palestinians with access to Israelis in the dialogue, appeared to grow in self-confidence, but also became more resentful and angrier about their relative deprivation.

Facts on the Ground

As illustrated in Chapter 5, over time the facts, that is the architecture of the occupation, have evolved and they keep changing. For the Israelis these 'facts' are about their security, while for the Palestinians they are about oppression.

When the Israeli survey respondents were asked what the Palestinians want now, several non-Olive Tree Israelis said that many would like to expel or exterminate Jewish Israelis. Only the 'realistic' Palestinians, they said, have grasped that this is impossible and might thereby settle for less than they aspire to, in order to have peace. None of the non-Olive Tree Israelis mentioned what the Palestinian survey respondents themselves said they wanted. By contrast, all the Olive Tree Israelis reported what their Palestinian counterparts explained they wanted, that is: an end to occupation, freedom, independence, a state, normal lives, equal rights, and/or the 'Right of Return' for Palestinian refugees.

Asked what the Israelis want now, there was no consensus among the non-Olive Tree Israelis. Some said the Israelis want separation from the Palestinians and/or a two-state compromise. Others said the Israelis want a continuation of the occupation plus an end to Palestinian violence. Others simply said they want peace if only that were possible.

Olive Tree Israelis reported that most Israelis want the continuation of the status quo plus respect and acceptance internationally, including an end to boycotts and divestment. Some volunteered that Israelis in general are in denial about the occupation and the deprivation of Palestinian rights.

In answer to the question: 'What do the Palestinians want now?' the non-Olive Tree Palestinian respondents listed: safety, an end to occupation,

rights, freedom and justice. The Right of Return for refugees was also mentioned. The Olive Tree Palestinians responded similarly, with the emphasis on
freedom rather than safety, and, they said, 'the same as what the Israelis want
for themselves'. One Olive Tree Palestinian did say she had to be realistic and
would settle for a formula that would 'end the violence'.

There was little if any difference between how the Olive Tree and the
non-Olive Tree Palestinian respondents depicted what the Israelis want now.
Basically, they said they want it all, the continuation of the occupation and an
end to violence. In their answers there was no expectation that the Israelis were
looking for a compromise deal with the Palestinians.

The message here is that Israelis can come to understand how fundamental
a grievance the occupation (and blockade of Gaza) is for all the Palestinians.
Meanwhile, both Israelis and Palestinians described 'the other' as wanting to do
them harm.

The Peace Business and 'Oslo' in Particular

As recounted in Chapter 6, when asked whether there were any other actors
involved in the conflict, aside from the Israelis and Palestinians, all the Israeli
respondents said yes and named many. The Olive Tree Israeli respondents saw
the roles of these other actors in more negative terms than the non-Olive Tree
Israeli respondents. The Palestinians also said there were many other actors involved and all of them saw that involvement as largely negative. The Palestinians
proved much more conscious of the contemporary roles of the United States
and the EU than did the Israelis.

With respect to the Oslo Accords, the non-Olive Tree Israelis thought the
process these engendered had fallen short of the goals in not producing peace.
However, they thought 'Oslo' had at least introduced a representative body for
the Palestinians and autonomy for them in parts of the West Bank. In this sense
they thought it had been beneficial for the Palestinians.

The Olive Tree Israelis were more nuanced in their appraisal of the 'Oslo
process'. They said it denoted recognition, or acknowledgement at least, of the
Palestinians as a people. Yet they also noted that its effect had been to relieve
the Israelis of the need to run the daily lives of the Palestinians. Several of them
blamed Israeli hardliners for the failures of Oslo.

Palestinian views on the Oslo process were profoundly negative. As they
said, it was a total failure 'for us' and it had brought poverty, unemployment,

checkpoints, settlements and 'the security situation' (i.e. Palestinian insecurity). It also served the Israelis, they believed, by subcontracting management of the occupation to the Palestinian Authority.

The Olive Tree Palestinians were less fixated on the specifics of the infrastructure and security operations emanating from Oslo, and more concerned with how Oslo served Israeli and Zionist ambitions.

One of the messages here is that the Israelis generally had no idea how the Oslo process – including the creation of the Palestinian Authority – is regarded by the Palestinians and in the Israeli narrative it is depicted as a concession to and benefit for the Palestinians.

What Now?

The final question I put to the survey respondents, as discussed in Chapter 7, was: 'What should happen now?' The answers of those who had not participated in the Olive Tree Programme demonstrated a complete absence of consensus on the Israeli side and a desire for revolution on the Palestinian side.

What was particularly interesting was the lack of consensus about what should happen now *even* among Israelis of similar background. Even so, all the comparator group Israelis responded to this question prescriptively and with confidence. Broadly, their proposals took into account what they thought the main obstacles to peace were on both sides, but deduced from these that the onus was on the Palestinians to settle for less than they presumed they aspired to. The need to reassure the Israeli public that their security would be protected featured in their responses. Some of them acknowledged that their preferences for what should happen would not necessarily be acceptable to a majority of Israelis and certainly not to many of them.

In so far as they did foresee insuperable problems, however, these had more to do with their perceptions of the Palestinians than of their fellow Israelis. By contrast, in their responses, the Olive Tree Israelis indicated palpable anxiety about what they saw as the trends in their own society. Crucially also, these Israelis were not prescriptive. On the contrary, they professed great uncertainty about what could or should be done, fearing that too many Israelis were either in denial about the needs and rights of the Palestinians or did not care. They expected the occupation to continue because, in Israeli security terms, it was manageable and preferable to dramatic change.

Among the non-Olive Tree Palestinians, unexpectedly, there was also a sense that they needed to sort themselves out first, before they could contemplate changing bilateral relations. In fact, they advocated revolution in the Palestinian body politic. They wanted the abolition of the Palestinian Authority, an end to corruption, the replacement of the 'old guard' of Palestinian leaders with better educated youth and they called for unity between the West Bank and Gaza Strip.

The Olive Tree Palestinian respondents did not call for a revolution, but they did see a need for fundamental change on the Palestinian side. Neither in their case nor that of the non-Olive Tree Palestinians, was this call for change of a nature likely to conform with Israeli wishes. The kind of change they wanted was one that would enable the Palestinians to fight more effectively for an end to occupation. That and 'justice', as opposed to 'victory', as one Olive Tree Palestinian put it, was what was called for. They also saw a need for societal healing and education, along with an end to suppression and deprivation, for fear of a total breakdown of order on the Palestinian side.

Meanwhile, they offered few if any prescriptions for how to resolve the conflict and they expected the Israelis to prefer continuation of the occupation rather than its end. Even so, the Olive Tree Palestinians did identify increasing divisions within Israeli society and believed that a breakdown in social cohesion was immanent on the Israeli side.

Thus, both the Palestinian and the Israeli Olive Tree alumni worried most about social and political trends in the two societies. They did not invest much if any hope in the array of formulae for a peace deal advocated by successive generations of international peacemakers, though some of them thought the international community could do more to help them.

Research Findings Overall

Absent intervention or a change in the circumstances of the individuals involved in the conflict, the general pattern was as follows:

- Each national group defines itself in contrast or juxtaposition to the other and attributes malign motives to the other.
- Each national group operates within its own narrative and sees no reason to question the way its narrative interprets the facts.
- Each national group places the onus on the other to make the changes it considers necessary for ending the conflict.
- Each national group believes its cause is more legitimate than that of

the other.

- Israelis think the 'Oslo process' made the situation of the Palestinians better and Palestinians think it made their situation worse.
- Palestinians want first and foremost an end to the occupation and the blockade of Gaza, freedom and rights, irrespective of how this is accomplished, but Israelis assume they want a whole range of things detrimental to the Israelis.

However, given the chance:

- Israelis and Palestinians can discern how their respective national narratives enshrine their respective identities and justify group behaviour on the basis of contrary interpretations of the facts. This realisation may cause them to reconsider their personal options.
- It is possible for Israelis to revise their assumptions about what the Palestinians want now – that is an end to occupation – as opposed to revenge and/or the elimination of Israel.
- It is possible for Israelis to understand the Palestinian national cause as legitimate and in competition with their own, yet in doing so they confess to an increased sense of insecurity.
- It is possible for Palestinians and Israelis to discover that entering into cross-conflict dialogue, under certain circumstances, can increase their understanding of the conflict without undermining their commitment to their national identity.

Overall, I would contend, the survey confirmed that the two sides have internalized national narratives about themselves and the other which militate against seeing the other as equal. The survey results also bore out the discoveries made by the Olive Tree Programme participants about the role of their respective narratives in driving and deepening the conflict. They showed how each side regards the other as undermining the prospects of peace by their very nature.

Further, the survey demonstrated how even an exercise in cross-conflict dialogue, over three years and away from the conflict zone, cannot cause the conflict protagonists to change fundamentally how they understand themselves. The Palestinians became even more conscious of the freedoms they lack and they did not 'buy' Israeli explanations for how this had come about as justification. There was more change on the Israeli side, as a result of 'talking to the enemy,' in so far as some Israelis felt more urgently the need to question the morality of the occupation and see its continuance as potentially corrosive for their own cause.

One may also deduce from the research that the occupation is now the central issue in the conflict. An end to this and the realisation of equal national and individual rights for both nationalities would therefore appear fundamental to a solution. Yet, as the research also indicates, for this to come about would require both sides to let go of their negative characterisations of the other. However, the Israelis are in a superior position to the Palestinians and the latter are stuck with a definition of themselves as the subjects of occupation.

Before turning to the general conclusions to be drawn here, I believe it is in order to say a little more about the effect of the Olive Tree on those who participated in the Programme.

The 'Olive Tree Effect'

It is commonly assumed that any cross-conflict dialogue exercise must be a good thing and that, at the grassroots level, it can help prepare the ground for peace. As explained in Chapter 1, however, the evidence suggests otherwise. At the level of civil society, dialogue can and frequently does reinforce antagonistic group identities. In most cases it will be used by the participants to pursue the conflict through argument and/or reinforce their assumptions about the enemy. This is because, in the absence of determined political leadership and commitment to sustainable peace, ordinary people cannot change the power balance (or imbalance) at the state or societal level.

That said, what 'talking to the enemy' can do, *provided* it is conducted as a purely exploratory exercise, and takes place in a setting conducive to learning and at a distance from the battleground, is expose 'the narrative trap' for examination. That was demonstrated in the case of the Olive Tree, which was instructive, but only for those directly involved, and only in so far as it helped them realise the role of the narratives in driving the conflict. So then the question becomes: 'So what?'

The answer, as alluded to already, is that the Olive Tree had value in two respects. First, it yielded the insights recounted in this book, from which, it is hoped, others may learn. Second it enabled the actual participants to gain degrees, thereby improve their career prospects *and* identify new possibilities for how they, as individuals, could proceed in the rest of their lives. So they, I maintain, did benefit personally, even though, regrettably, such opportunities are unlikely ever to be made available on a grand scale to others in their respective societies.

As discussed in more depth in the previous chapter, both the Israelis and the Palestinians awarded Olive Tree scholarships arrived at a far more nuanced, thoughtful and tempered appraisal of their situation than they had started with. They had let go of their binary, black versus white narratives, and accepted complexity as preferable to denial and dualism.

In their own words, this is how four of the alumni encapsulated what they gained from the experience:

Two Palestinian reflections:

- The experience I will remember most was growing personally and becoming more in contact with my own agency. I learned quite a big deal. How to listen, argue, debate, and not to be threatened by the existence of a different opinion.

- I have learned a lot about the conflict, the other and myself. I learned how to be patient, willing to listen and contain and control myself, my thoughts and my feelings. I feel empowered and inspired.

And two Israeli reflections:

- The '48 presentation in the first year was very meaningful to me. I had to ask friends of mine about their narrative of the '48 war. When I saw their answers, I felt like I really don't want to present it because it might hurt the Palestinians in the group. This was the first time that I felt a conflict between the ideas I grew up on and the fact that I have Palestinian friends.

- I learnt that my home is much more complicated than I thought (and I assumed it was quite complex to begin with); that some of the stories can never quite fit in together; and that it is possible to get some of the facts right, and still disagree on their meaning. I think being a part of this group, in which each individual is weird in a different and unique way, made me a more open and empathetic person.

The Wider Implications of the Findings

Returning to the general points made at the beginning of this chapter, the key message of this work is that identity conflicts are not only about 'the facts', they are also about how those facts feature and are interpreted in the contending group narratives.

When these narratives not only tell the group members who they are and who they are not, but also construct definitions of self and other which denigrate and blame 'the other' for the problems they face, the narratives become conflict drivers. They permit and encourage resort to force against those not recognised as members of the in-group. Herein lies one facet of that I am calling 'the narrative trap', violence tends to beget more violence.

The other facet of this trap derives from the way the narratives define identity. If a group member chooses to question the way the narrative interprets the facts and considers the possibility that the narrative description of the enemy is in some way flawed, they risk rejection and denigration by members of their own group. Their judgement is questioned, their motives become suspect and they can expect to be attacked for their views. If they claim that they are only trying to hold up a mirror to their own community and establish whether they are acting in the best interests of that group or nation, they will be received as criticising their compatriots and impugning *their* motives and judgement.

The trap is that a critic of the prevailing narrative may thereby be forced to choose between their group belonging and their personal reading of 'the facts'. The consequences of separating from the rest of the group may be diminished career prospects, demotion, isolation or worse. As Albert Camus framed it, they may find themselves faced with a choice between toeing the line to keep food on their family's table and adhering to their principles. Loyalty to a group may be at odds with commitment to so-called universalist values of human equality and individual rights.

Whether or not there is a dilemma will depend on the circumstances. When a group is at risk, such as when threatened with attack or invasion, or a people are systematically discriminated against or subjugated, few group members will see a dilemma. The problem occurs, however, when, a group is not systematically disadvantaged and, for their own purposes, a leader seeks to mobilise the group for action by exploiting their fears. Since group narratives are constructed in ways that appeal to the emotions of group members, rather than their objectivity, they can be manipulated.

These observations have traction in the context of the Israeli-Palestinian conflict, but not exclusively so. They are offered here as a demonstration of what can happen when we let an exclusivist version of our group or national narrative take us over.

Acknowledgements

It is to the Palestinian and Israeli men and women who committed their time, focus and engagement to the Olive Tree cross-conflict dialogue that I owe the biggest debt of gratitude for the discoveries recounted in this book. Without them, it would not exist, and I personally would not have learned so much about conflict narratives and how to discern them. In what they have accomplished since, they remain an enduring source of inspiration.

For their roles in the genesis and development of the ideas underpinning this work I would like to thank Damian Gorman, Dr Anton Obholzer, Dr Kathleen Jordan, Dr Julia Amos, Dr Tarak Barkawi, Charlotte Halvorsen, Andrea Kenneally and Dr James Rodgers. I am forever grateful to Damian, Anton, Julia, Charlotte and Andrea in particular for reviewing my analysis of the data collected, for their feedback and suggestions on successive drafts of the book and for their incredible support during the year it took me to draft and redraft the finished manuscript. I would also like to thank Dr Obholzer, Dr Barkawi and Dr Ian Black for their generous endorsements of the book and Dr Yoav Galai for his feedback on several chapters and permission to use his photographic work in the cover design.

I had the invaluable help of Ahmed Ziat and Nitzan Regev-Sanders in both the collection of the survey data and the translation of the responses from Arabic and Hebrew into English. The fieldwork involved was financed in part thanks to Mark Woodruff and the Mark Leonard Trust and to funding received by Dr Julia Amos, then at Merton College Oxford, from Peter J Braam, which I gratefully acknowledge. My profound thanks and appreciation go to Dr Khalil Shikaki and to Dr Mark Heller for enabling me to administer the survey to respondents in the Occupied Palestinian Territories and Israel respectively.

Finally, it is thanks to the expert guidance and support of Anthony Childs-Cutler and his team at Red Hawk Books, that the publication of this book has been realised with the seriousness befitting its message. Any mistakes or discrepancies that remain are my responsibility alone.

Commentaries on 'Surviving the Story'

This book takes a most complicated and wearisome subject that has bedevilled us for centuries and exposes it in its full complexity and history. Surprisingly and against a mass of learned academic papers, it comes up with a simple answer to the question, "How has this endless and stuck situation come about and what might be done to move towards resolution of all issues concerned in this political logjam?" Just as the expression, "It's the economy, stupid," became the cornerstone of understanding the voters' state of mind, the conclusion is obvious - namely, "It's the inner world, stupid."

With this answer, Professor Hollis turns the whole approach to the Israeli/Palestinian problem on its head, while meticulously and in great depth recording the process by which this was revealed. She makes the point that none of the so-called evidence that has been given, both external and emotional, have led to an understanding of the basic problems, nor has the capacity to intervene in a constructive way been revealed.

That is because the evidence or "facts," merely a "supernatant" layer, are accorded emphasis. It's the in-depth core layers which she calls "narratives" which are indeed the foundation stones of one's identity and broaching these has been found to be what is necessary.

As regards the basics of the narratives, psychologists and psychoanalysts will include amongst them intra-uterine and birth experiences and the inevitable perception of one's identity from the beginning of life – personal, family, group and societal.

No one in their right mind would think that everyday conscious experience solely in itself makes up the total reality of understanding their life. To paraphrase Nietzche, on the surface the swans seem to be swimming in a calm way but underneath the waterline they are paddling frantically to keep up with the underlying currents.

And so it is with this topic.

All the emphasis is on the everyday superficiality, such as one might see on the television, and none on the innermost realities of the early foundations. It is the seriousness of these original narratives which are key and need tackling before the other minor issues can be addressed. Not surprisingly Professor Hollis and her team therefore start by encouraging the participants in her seminars to begin with their narratives, before moving into the reality that each social grouping has its feet firmly clamped in its own societal narrative. Only after the acknowledgement that distinct social groupings have fundamentally different narratives, does the process of chipping away at differences begin.

Dr Anton Obholzer
Consultant Psychiatrist and Psychoanalyst, former Chief Executive of the Tavistock Centre.

———————

Some think conflicts exist primarily in our minds, while others imagine them as immutable clashes of national interest. In this penetrating study of cross-conflict dialogue, Rosemary Hollis weaves together with crystalline prose the sensibilities of a psychologist with those of the well-informed analyst of *realpolitik*. Using unique data from a university programme she directed for eight years, she shows us that getting to know our enemies leads to understanding but not to peace. Power asymmetries shape the everyday realities of Israelis and Palestinians, making concrete the myths and prejudices they hold about themselves and one another. In analyzing the narratives of Israeli and Palestinian students, Hollis offers us a clear-eyed and realistic model for a new generation of cross-conflict dialogues. Participants discover empowerment through reflection and learn to navigate their own paths through the conflict.

Tarak Barkawi
Professor of International Relations
London School of Economics and Political Science

———————

Rosemary Hollis is highly experienced in facilitating dialogue between Israelis and Palestinians – never an easy task. In this important and insightful work she draws on the evidence of exploratory learning exercises to enable deeper understanding between two peoples who have little choice but to live in the same contested land – and urgently need to acknowledge each other's rights.

Self-affirming national narratives, Hollis demonstrates, cannot be ignored as they, far more than hard facts, are the "drivers and life-blood" of this profoundly asymmetrical conflict. When Israelis talk about building a Jewish state Palestinians lament their statelessness and exile. Solutions are not guaranteed. But talking to the enemy and connecting between parallel universes is not only worthwhile but necessary.

The students from both sides who shared the safe and supportive space of the unique Olive Tree Programme at London's City University sometimes found their interactions uncomfortable and frustrating, especially during the repeated Gaza wars of recent years. Still, Palestinians and Israelis alike "arrived at a far more nuanced, thoughtful and tempered appraisal of their situation than they had started with," Hollis concludes – a valuable lesson from her years at the coalface of cross-conflict dialogue. "They had let go of their binary, black versus white narratives, and accepted complexity as preferable to denial and dualism. That said, they both saw inequality, and the occupation that enforced, as the root problem dragging both societies into crisis."

Ian Black, author of *Enemies and Neighbours: Arabs and Jews in Palestine and Israel, 1917-2017*

Lightning Source UK Ltd.
Milton Keynes UK
UKHW010712290919
350673UK00007B/194/P